RECENT LITERATURE

ON

INTEREST

(1884–1899)

A SUPPLEMENT TO "CAPITAL AND INTEREST"

BY

EUGENE v. BÖHM-BAWERK

AUSTRIAN MINISTER OF FINANCE, AND HONORARY PROFESSOR OF POLITICAL ECONOMY IN THE UNIVERSITY OF VIENNA

TRANSLATED BY

WILLIAM A. SCOTT, PH.D.

DIRECTOR OF THE SCHOOL OF COMMERCE AND PROFESSOR OF ECONOMIC HISTORY AND THEORY IN THE UNIVERSITY OF WISCONSIN

AND

PROFESSOR DOCTOR SIEGMUND FEILBOGEN

UNIVERSITÄTS-DOCENT IN THE UNIVERSITY OF VIENNA

New York

THE MACMILLAN COMPANY

LONDON: MACMILLAN & CO., LTD.

1903

Set up, electrotyped, and published September, 1903.

Norwood Press
J. S. Cushing & Co. — Berwick & Smith Co.
Norwood, Mass., U.S.A.

TRANSLATOR'S PREFACE

This little volume is intended as a supplement to the admirable translation of the first edition of Professor Böhm-Bawerk's "Geschichte und Kritik der Capitalzins-Theorien," given to the world by Professor William Smart of Glasgow in 1890. During the twelve years since this notable contribution to the critical literature of economic science has been available to English-speaking students, great progress has been made in the realm of economic theory, and for this Böhm-Bawerk and Professor Smart's translation are in no slight degree responsible. Whatever may be the final verdict of science regarding the agio theory, no one can doubt that the splendid example of criticism and analysis which is contained in Böhm-Bawerk's work has raised theoretical discussion to a higher level and has been a constant and powerful stimulus to investigation in this field.

In the United States the appearance of Smart's translation must be regarded as an event of prime importance in the history of political economy. The work of some of our theorists[1] had already been directed along practically the same line as that of Jevons and the Austrians, and a new generation of young economists had just entered the field. Böhm-Bawerk's masterly treatise gave support and encouragement to the former, and guidance and stimulus to the latter. It has been discussed over and over again in the courses in economic theory and in the economic seminaries of the country, and it is safe to say that no candidate for the doctorate in economics during the last twelve years has been absolved from the requirement of familiarizing himself with this work.

Abundant proof of Böhm-Bawerk's influence is furnished by our literature. A glance at the files of the *Political Science Quarterly*, the *Quarterly Journal of Economics*, and the *Annals* indicates that a large proportion of

[1] Notably Professor John B. Clark and Professor Simon N. Patten.

the articles treating of economic theory are either directly upon some phase of Böhm-Bawerk's work or theories, or have been clearly influenced, if not directly inspired, by them. Of the books on economic theory which have appeared during the last twelve years, not one that I can recall fails to take account of his work, and few, if any, of them fail to show the effects of his influence. It is impossible to say as much as this of any other book or any other man. Great as has been Marshall's influence, it has not approximated Böhm-Bawerk's either in scope or intensity.

In 1900 the second edition of the "Geschichte und Kritik der Capitalzins-Theorien" appeared, and the present volume contains in its nine main chapters a translation of the Appendix, in which Böhm-Bawerk reviews the literature on interest which had appeared since 1884, the date to which the first edition translated by Smart brought the subject. In this preface we propose to give a summary of the most important of the other additions contained in the second edition. These are the author's Preface, chapter XI on John Rae, and a supplement to the chapter on Karl Marx. To the author and the translators it has not seemed necessary or desirable to present a complete translation of these less important additions. A brief summary is sufficient to indicate their general character and scope, and the English-speaking reader who is unfamiliar with German and who desires more may avail himself of Miss Alice M. Macdonald's translation[1] of Böhm-Bawerk's criticism of the posthumous volumes of Karl Marx's "Das Kapital," of the author's reply to Walker's strictures in the *Quarterly Journal of Economics*,[2] and of Rae's book itself.[3]

The Preface of the second edition treats

[1] "Karl Marx and the Close of his System." A Criticism by Eugene v. Böhm-Bawerk. Translated by Alice M. Macdonald, with a preface by James Bonar, M.A., LL.D. London, T. Fisher Unwin, Paternoster Square, 1898.

[2] "The Positive Theory of Capital and its Critics." *Quarterly Journal of Economics*, April, 1895.

[3] "Statement of some new principles on the subject of Political Economy, exposing the fallacies of the system of free trade, and of some other doctrines maintained in the 'Wealth of Nations.'" Boston, 1834.

chiefly of the author's defence of his method against the strictures of Alfred Marshall and of the late Francis A. Walker. These men had charged Böhm-Bawerk with misinterpreting many of the authors whom he criticised in "Capital and Interest," claiming that he frequently mistook "blunders of expression" for errors of judgment. Walker was a firm adherent of the productivity theory, and was unable to believe that any really able thinker could have sought for an explanation of interest in any other direction. He, therefore, denied the separate existence of the abstinence and the use theories. He claimed that the authors of these so-called theories intended them only as "a social justification of interest," and did not themselves mistake them for adequate explanations of the causes of this phenomenon. In this connection he mentioned especially Hermann, Karl Menger, and Senior.

Professor Marshall finds the explanation of interest in the coöperation of what he calls the "productiveness" and the 'prospectiveness" of capital, the former determining the demand for that factor of production, and the latter limiting the supply. He believes that most of the writers on interest have had both these elements of the problem in mind, and have differed from each other chiefly in the fact that some have laid more emphasis upon the one element, and others upon the other. He has expressed the opinion that many of the authors criticised by Böhm-Bawerk would not have accepted his statements as fair and complete presentations of their views.[1]

In reply, Böhm-Bawerk says that the question at issue between himself and such critics as Walker and Marshall does not so much concern the interpretation and estimation of the views of other authors as the real essence of the interest problem, and the requirements for its solution. Regarding what the authors criticised really meant, he is quite willing to leave the decision to the intelligent readers of his book, for whose benefit he has very often quoted their exact words; but in justification of his view of the nature of the problem of interest, and the conditions necessary for its

[1] "Principles of Economics," 3d ed., pp. 142–664.

solution, he submits some characteristic statements of Walker and Marshall to analysis and criticism.

He disposes of Walker in a single paragraph. Referring to his statement regarding the teachings of Hermann, Menger, and Senior that "they thus reached a social justification of interest which no one of them probably ever mistook for a scientific ascertainment of the cause of interest," and that on account of their "blunders in expression" Böhm-Bawerk ascribed to them independent, deeply thought-out theories which they never held, our author says: "I do not think that I need waste a single word to prove that, on the contrary, it would have been most ungenerous, and for a true historian absolutely impossible, to have simply obliterated the use and abstinence theories from the history of the development of interest theories and to have drawn the old story of the productivity theory from the most widely differing methods of explanation, or, more accurately, to have forced that interpretation upon them."

The criticism of Marshall bears upon two

points chiefly. In Böhm-Bawerk's opinion he overestimates the explanatory power of the coöperation of "productiveness" and "prospectiveness," and is deceived regarding the actual relation in which the different groups of theories stand to this coöperation. On the first point Böhm-Bawerk refers to a passage in the chapter on the eclectics, in which he says that no impartial observer could fail to see that interest is in some way connected with the productivity of capital, and with the abstinence required for saving, but such an observation, he says, comes far short of an explanation of interest. It may be compared to the observation that a rainbow appears whenever the sun strikes a rain-cloud at a certain angle. No one would regard this as a scientific explanation of the rainbow. It is the duty of science to point out the exact connection between this apparent cause and its effects, and the explanation would be very different according as the scientist assumed the undulatory or the emission theory of light. In like manner, "productiveness" and "prospectiveness" furnish no explanation of interest. They constitute only the framework of an explanation. The problem is to show the connection between these facts and interest.

The injustice of Marshall's charges and his evident misunderstanding of Böhm-Bawerk's real attitude toward the authors he criticises is further shown by reference to certain passages in the first edition in which our author pointed out the affinity between the use and the productivity theories. In one place[1] he called the former an offshoot of the latter, and in another[2] he said: "This theory [the use theory] assumes capital to be productive." Again, on page 187, he said: "The relation of use theories to the productive power of capital will not, however, be found stated so clearly in the writings of their representatives as I have thought necessary to state it. On the contrary, indeed, appeals to the productive power of capital long accompany the development of the use theory proper, and we are very often left in doubt whether the author relies, for his explanations of surplus value, more on the productive power of capital or on the arguments peculiar to the use theory."

[1] Smart's translation, p. 185. [2] *Ibid.*, p. 186.

Marshall reproaches our author for having failed to credit some of the naive-productivity theorists with a recognition of the significance of abstinence in the explanation of interest. In reply, Böhm-Bawerk affirms that he noted every express utterance of the most important writers of this group indicative of such recognition; for example, of J. B. Say, Roscher, Rossi, Leroy-Beaulieu, Cauwés, and others. He adds that he classed as eclectics those writers who combine the distinct and explicit recognition of sacrifice and abstinence with positive assertions of the independent value-creating power of capital, but insists that there are writers belonging to the "naive-productivity" group who do not accompany their emphatic assertions of the independent productivity of capital with any allusion to the concurrent influence of sacrifice or "prospectiveness," and that he would have been unjust to these authors and unfaithful to history if he had assumed that they recognized such an influence. "I believe," he says, "that a certain tendency of thinking, once rather popular, though at present entirely obsolete, led to the belief that the theoretical problem of interest could be perfectly explained by reference to the independent, value-creating power of capital, and that this tendency occupies a middle position in point of time between the old physiocratic view of the exclusive, value-creating power of land and the more recent socialistic doctrine, now on the road to destruction, of the exclusive, value-creating power of labour, and is allied to both these ideas." He would, therefore, have been unjust to history if he had failed to point out this tendency. He would have been unjust to the writers he discussed if he had criticised them for views which he assumed, without direct evidence and sometimes even against indirect evidence, that they held. He concludes with the statement that in his opinion Marshall would not have brought against him the charges to which he has been making a reply "had not unfortunately the extraordinary clearness and exactness which is habitual to him in the conception and working out of his theoretical ideas failed him in that part of his most excellent work devoted to the subject of capital."

Next to the Appendix here translated on the recent literature of interest, the most important addition to the second edition is the chapter on John Rae inserted between the chapters on the labour and the exploitation theories. Rae clearly anticipated some of Böhm-Bawerk's ideas, though this fact was not known to the latter at the time of the publication of the first edition, and in this chapter, which contains an excellent summary and criticism of Rae's work, this fact is clearly recognized, and the precise points anticipated explained.

John Rae was a Scotchman who emigrated to Canada, and in 1834 wrote a book which was published in Boston and entitled "Statement of some new principles on the subject of Political Economy, exposing the fallacies of the system of free trade, and some other doctrines maintained in the 'Wealth of Nations.'" As the title implies, the book was written primarily for the purpose of pointing out the inapplicability of Adam Smith's free trade doctrines to Canada, and does not seem to have attracted much attention among the economists of that time. John Stuart Mill (Bk. I, Ch. XI) made some quotations from it, and in a note expressed a high opinion of the author and his work. In 1856 this book was translated into Italian and published as Volume XI of the "Biblioteca dell' Economista," but Italian economists do not seem to have read it extensively. At any rate, Luigi Cossa in his "Introduzione allo studio dell' Economia Politica" devotes but five lines to it, in which it becomes evident that his knowledge of it was derived from Mill and not from the book itself. In view of these facts and the scarcity of the book in Germany, it is not surprising that Böhm-Bawerk had not read it at the time of the publication of his first edition. His attention was called to the importance of this work by C. W. Mixter's article in the *Quarterly Journal of Economics* for January, 1897, entitled "A Forerunner of Böhm-Bawerk," and Professor Karl Menger placed a copy of the book at his disposal.

Rae's book is divided into three parts, the first treating of the lack of identity between the interests of individuals and nations, the second of "the nature of stock and the laws governing its increase and diminution," and the third, "of the operations of the legislator on natural stock." Part II contains fifteen of the twenty-two chapters, and two hundred and eighty of the three hundred and eighty-seven pages of the book, and it is to this part that Böhm-Bawerk devotes his analysis and criticism in the chapter here under consideration.

Rae begins his exposition of the nature of stock by describing production as a process of fashioning or manipulating the "materials" of nature into "instruments" which shall produce "events" in the future. The objects of men's desires, or the means of satisfying their wants, are "mere arrangements of matter," and all the combinations or manipulations of materials made by men for this purpose he terms "instruments." "In general, then," he says on page 87, "all those changes which man makes in the form or arrangement of the parts of material objects, for the purpose of supplying his future wants, and which derive their power of doing this from his knowledge of the course of events, and the changes which his labour, guided by his reason, is hence enabled to make in the issue of these events, may be termed instruments."

This description of the nature and purposes of production bears considerable resemblance to Böhm-Bawerk's treatment of the subject in the early chapters of the "Positive Theory," in which he describes "goods," their "material services," and the functions of capital. Rae's conception of "instruments" and Böhm-Bawerk's conception of capital or "intermediate goods," however, are not identical, as the latter shows in a footnote on pages 379, 380, but they have much in common.

Rae next describes the common features of these instruments. "They are all," he says, "*directly* formed by human labour, or *indirectly* through the aid of other instruments themselves formed by human labour;" they all "bring to pass, or tend, or help, to bring to pass events supplying some of the wants of man, and are then exhausted;" and a space of time intervenes between their formation and their exhaustion. The power of instruments to bring events to pass, or the amount of goods they can produce, is termed their "capacity." A proper measure of this, in Rae's opinion, is the amount of labour for which the returns of the instruments will exchange, this amount being measured by the wages rather than the sacrifices of labour. He adds that a comparison of the capacities of different instruments belonging to the same class, that is, contributing to the satisfaction of the same category of wants, may be made on the basis of their relative physical effects, as, for example, the relative heating power of different woods.

Rae then classifies instruments according to the advantages or profits which may be derived from their ownership. This involves a comparison of the cost of their production in labour, of the amount of their returns or product, and of the length of time intervening between the formation of the instruments and their exhaustion. The relation between these three factors is indicated by arranging the instruments in orders or series "determined by the period of time at which instruments placed in them issue (or would issue if not before exhausted) in events equivalent to double the labour expended in forming them." Thus instruments belonging to series A will yield a return equal to double their cost in one year, those in series B in two years, in series C in three years, etc.

The most important part of Rae's exposition now follows, in which he explains the causes and the laws of the increase and decrease of the instruments of a society. The former are said to be four in number: (1) "The quantity and quality of the materials owned by it;" (2) "the strength of the *effective desire of accumulation;*" (3) "the rate of wages;" and (4) "the progress of the inventive faculty." Of these the second and fourth receive the major portion of attention, and in their discussion Rae reveals the points of chief importance in his theory of capital and interest. As a preliminary to this discussion he attempts to establish the following proposition: "The capacity which any people can communicate to the materials they possess, by forming them into instruments, cannot be indefinitely increased, while their knowledge of their powers and qualities remains stationary, without moving the instruments formed continually onwards in the series A, B, C, etc.; but there is no assignable limit to the extent of the capacity which a people, having attained considerable knowledge of the qualities and powers of the materials they possess, can communicate to them without carrying them out of series A, B, C, etc., even if that knowledge remain stationary."

The first part of this law is established by the following process of reasoning: The capacity of instruments can be increased by making them more durable or by increasing their efficiency. In the first case a larger amount of labour must be expended in their production, and, even if this new labour adds as much to their productive power as that previously expended, the returns are moved farther off in time, and in consequence the instruments are pushed down to a lower series. To increase the efficiency of an instrument likewise requires the expenditure of more labour, since instruments of greater efficiency can only be obtained by the manipulation of scarcer or more refractory materials. The increased cost thus necessitated forces the instruments into a lower series. In proof of the second part of the law Rae mentions the almost innumerable combinations of productive powers and materials possible in nations whose knowledge of nature and of technique is extensive. Under such circumstances the movement toward the lower series is slow and there is no assignable limit to the quantity of instruments that may be produced with profit. The question of the increase of instruments of production, therefore, becomes one of technique or knowledge of natural forces and materials and the methods of manipulating them on the one hand, and of the extent to which a people will be willing to carry the process of producing instruments of lower and lower series on the other; that is, of what Rae calls "the progress of the inventive faculty," and the "effective desire of accumulation." The former increases the number of instruments which may be produced without greatly increasing the number of lower series, and the latter determines the remoteness of the future period for which a people are willing to provide by the sacrifice of present labour or its equivalent.

Rae's analysis of the circumstances which determine the effective desire for accumulation brings him to the discussion of the relation between present and future enjoyments. Most men, he says, discount future pleasures, partly on account of the uncertainty and shortness of life, and partly on account of their inability to realize the future. Their intellectual qualities and their "social and benevolent affections" are, therefore, elements in the problem. The stronger the former are, the more keenly they appreciate future needs, and the less liable are they to be influenced by the passions of the moment; the stronger is their interest in and their affection for others, the greater their desire to influence events in the future. The growth of family and social ties, the development of the moral powers of a people, and the improvement of all those conditions, social, political, and economic, which increase the probability that we ourselves, or those for whom we care, will be permitted in the future to enjoy the results of our present sacrifices, are calculated to strengthen the effective desire for accumulation.

From this discussion Rae proceeds to the subject of the division of labour and exchange. He sees the advantages of the former in the fact that when a worker devotes himself to one branch of production, instruments are more continuously used and more quickly exhausted, and hence are raised to higher and more productive series. Their increase and accumulation thus become more profitable, and the effective desire for accumulation is increased. This method of viewing the advantages of the division of labour is considered so important by Rae that he devotes a special appendix to its defence, and to a criticism of Adam Smith's treatment of the subject.

The discussion of the division of labour and of exchange leads to a consideration of value which he explains in accordance with the cost of reproduction theory, to which, however, he makes one important and very significant addition. "When two persons in the same society exchange commodities," he says (p. 300), ". . . the exchanges they make are for equal quantities of labour, *reckoned according to the time when applied, and the actual order of instruments.*"[1] The time element, to which attention is called in this last clause, is considered by

[1] The italics are mine.

Rae of equal importance with labour. Materials, tools, etc., as well as labour, are consumed in production, and they must be represented in the price of the goods. In this connection he shows that not only the labour which produced these instruments must be taken into consideration, but also the length of time that must elapse before that labour is remunerated. The rate of compensation for this element of time will depend upon the effective desire for accumulation. By way of illustration, he assumes the case of a weaver who can weave a certain amount of thread into linen in thirty days with the aid of a loom which cost one hundred days' labour and which will last seven years. He then proceeds as follows: "Suppose that the effective desire of accumulation of the individual is of strength sufficient to carry him to the order *G*, doubling in seven years, that the loom cost one hundred days' labour, and that it will be exhausted in seven years; it would then require to return two hundred days' labour, or an equivalent, at the end of that period. The return, however, is not delayed so long, but begins to come in daily, immediately after its construction. Calculating then what yearly return is equal to two hundred days at the end of seven years, in the estimation of a man who reckons one day now equal to two then, it will turn out to be nearly twenty days. We may allow that the loom is in employment three hundred days a year; it would, therefore, on these principles, have to return two days' labour for every thirty days during which it was in operation, and the weaver would consequently have to receive an equivalent to thirty-two days' labour; at least, had he not a moral certainty of receiving this, he would not have formed the instrument, and were such return to cease, he would not reconstruct it" (pp. 169, 170).

Farther on he adds that "even in cases where labour alone seems to be paid for, the time generally also forms one of the items to be taken into account. Thus an individual contracts to fell the trees on a certain piece of forest land in a North American settlement within three months. If then he be paid at the commencement of the three months, he will expect to receive less than if payment be deferred until the expiration of that time, and the difference between the two amounts will be regulated, as in other cases, by the particular orders to which instruments, in that particular situation, are generally wrought up. The same thing holds good in all instances where labour is paid for by the work executed, or, as it is termed, by the piece."

The same idea appears in another passage in which the difference between the valuation placed upon present and future goods of the same kind and amount is expressed in a striking manner. After stating that all instruments possess a capacity for supplying wants or saving labour, he adds: "But the wants which they supply, and the labour which they save, are in general not immediate, but future. Now we cannot estimate the same amount of labour saved, or wants supplied, to-morrow, and five or fifty years hence, as equivalent, the one to the other. Thus, if we compare together a hundred full-grown trees, and as many saplings, it may be that, estimated in the supply they yield the wants of futurity, they are alike.

If the former be cut down to-morrow, they may yield a hundred cords of fire-wood, and if the latter be cut down fifty years hence, they may yield the same. We should not, nevertheless, conceive that they were equal the one to the other. What measure, then, are we to adopt for comparing them and other such instruments together, and thus finding an expression in a quantity of immediate labour for the whole capacity of instruments possessed by any community or for the whole stock of that community? The natural measure would seem to be the relative estimate, which the individuals concerned themselves form of the present and the future, that is, the strength of the effective desire of accumulation of the particular commodity. Thus in a community whose effective desire of accumulation is of a strength sufficient to carry it to the formation of instruments of the order E, doubling in five years, an instrument, which at the expiration of five years yielded a return equivalent to two days' labour, might fairly be estimated as equivalent to one day's present labour; if at the expiration of ten years it yielded an equivalent to four days' labour, it might also now be rated at one day's labour, and so for other periods" (pp. 171, 172).

In this connection Böhm-Bawerk calls attention to the fact that Rae has given us two methods of measuring the influence of the time element upon value, the one being the strength of the effective desire for accumulation, and the other the productivity of the lowest order of instruments produced by the society in question. That these two measures are not identical is recognized by Rae himself in a statement in which he distinguishes between cases "where the effective desire of accumulation of a community has had opportunity to work up the materials possessed by it into instruments of an order corresponding to its own strength," and those "where the accumulative principle has not yet had time fully to operate." (See pp. 172 sq., 194, 264.)

Böhm-Bawerk claims that the latter is the normal condition of things, because certain circumstances, among which are the new discoveries which play so important a rôle in Rae's exposition, prevent the complete realization of the effects of the psychological facts referred to in the expression "the effective desire of accumulation."

The longest chapter in Rae's book treats "of the causes of the progress of invention and of the effects arising from it." This subject is treated historically, and in a very interesting manner. The most important points for the student of interest concern the way in which technical progress affects the magnitude of national wealth and the rate of interest.

The effect of discoveries is to reveal new or more suitable materials, or new qualities, or new methods of working in materials. The first effect of progress along this line is, therefore, to render labour more productive, and this effect in turn changes the relation between the capacity of instruments and the costs of their production, and thus transfers them to "more speedily returning orders," and increases the magnitude of the wealth of the nation. Improvements also raise the rate of profits, even if no change takes place in the effective desire for accumulation, since they increase the productivity of all instruments, and thus the returns of every series.

At the beginning of the critical part of his discussion, Böhm-Bawerk calls attention to the fact that Rae's chief interest was in the explanation of the causes of the increase of national wealth rather than of the rate of interest, and that in consequence he did not accord full treatment to many topics of importance in a discussion of the latter subject. In Rae's expressions on the interest problem our author discerns two different lines of thought, the one connecting interest with the influence which time exerts upon the estimation of needs and goods, and the other with certain facts connected with the technique of production. The difficulty of the problem, according to Böhm-Bawerk, consists in showing how these two elements coöperate in the determination of the rate of interest, and it is precisely here that Rae, as well as those of his successors who recognized the importance of both these elements, failed. Jevons, for example, did not attempt to combine them in his explanation, but adopted an eclectic method, explaining the external, technical facts connected with the productivity of capital after the manner of the productivity theory, and the psychological facts after the manner of the abstinence theory. Launhardt and Sax did not seem to feel the necessity of employing the former element in their explanation, but contented themselves with the use of the imperfect materials prepared but left unused by Jevons. Rae recognized the importance of both elements, but failed in his explanation of how they coöperate in the determination of interest. His treatment of this part of the subject may be summarized as follows: —

The fact that people estimate present goods more highly than future goods of the same quality and quantity explains the fact of interest. The rate depends upon the effective desire for accumulation on the one hand and certain facts concerning the technique of production on the other. If, for example, accumulation continues, while the state of knowledge remains stationary, the rate of interest must fall, because the use of materials of poorer quality increases the cost of production and thus diminishes the surplus which remains after deducting costs from product. The tendency is to carry accumulation to such a point that the surplus returns will correspond with the effective desire for accumulation. That such correspondence, however, is frequently not realized is explained by the fact that at times the community has not been able to work up the materials possessed by it into instruments corresponding to the strength of the accumulative principle. For this situation the "inventive principle" may be responsible. That is, new discoveries increase the "capacity" of instruments and raise them to a higher order of series, thus temporarily at least making it possible for people to discontinue the production of instruments of the lower degrees of capacity even when the strength of the effective desire for accumulation is great enough to warrant their production. In this manner Rae pushes the technical facts of production into the foreground of his explanation and the psychological factor into the background. The rate of interest is thus usually determined by the productivity of instruments, and only occasionally does it correspond with the actual strength of the effective desire for accumulation.

At this point Böhm-Bawerk calls attention to the fact that Rae's explanation is subject to the same criticism as the productivity theory. He confuses physical and value productivity, and the cause of this confusion seems to be the ambiguous use of the terms "capacity" and "returns." In his formal definitions and illustrations of "capacity" the purely technical conception is employed. For example, the capacity of a good is said to be great or small according as it helps to bring into existence many or few products. The capacity of an instrument can be increased either by lengthening its duration or by increasing the quantity of goods which it can produce in a given period of time. He illustrates the effects of inventions or improvements by the statement (p. 259) that with an improved form of plough, people can plough a larger piece of land with the same expenditure of human and animal labour. Rae then passes over to the conception of value productivity when he attempts to arrange instruments into series on the basis of the surplus they yield over costs. This he accomplishes by a comparison of the labour expended on the production of an instrument with the returns of that instrument, and as a measure of these two magnitudes he takes the value or the wages of the labour. Thus he compares the wages of the labour expended in the production of an instrument with the wages of the labour for which the returns or product of the instrument would exchange. In other words, he compares the value of the cost elements with the value of their product, the instrument, so-called, being the intermediate factor. He assumes that this comparison will reveal a surplus, the magnitude of which as compared with the value of the instrument determines the series to which the latter belongs. He then argues that this surplus is increased or decreased directly by changes in the physical productivity of instruments. For example, improvements or inventions make it possible to secure the same returns with less labour or greater returns with the same labour, and this, he argues, will increase the surplus due to the instrument in question, and will thus raise it to a higher series. The returns of which he speaks in the first part of the argument are concrete goods, but the surplus referred to is a surplus of value, obtained by subtracting the value of the cost elements from the value of these concrete goods. What he proves is that inventions increase the physical productivity of labour, and from that fact he draws the unwarranted conclusion that the value of the product and the value of the labour are farther apart than before. In like manner he explains the fall in the rate of interest due to increasing accumulations. These increasing accumulations, he argues, involve the use of materials of poorer quality or of materials more difficult to procure. Thus costs are increased. A given amount of labour yields a smaller return or a larger amount of labour is required to procure the same return. From this fact he draws the conclusion that the surplus due to the instrument in question must decrease. Thus from a decrease in the physical productivity of an instrument he argues a decreasing difference between the value of the instrument and that of its product.

Böhm-Bawerk also refers to the fact that Rae's reasoning is contradicted by his own doctrine of value. According to the cost of production theory, the value of the product ought to rise in the same proportion as the costs, and in that case no change in the surplus would be experienced. Rae also assumes throughout that the value of labour remains stationary, and that the sum of value represented by the costs increases and decreases only as the quantity of labour represented by it increases and decreases. He thus commits the fatal error of assuming that the forces which determine value operate upon the goods which constitute the returns, but has no influence whatever upon those which constitute costs.

After summarizing the similarities and the differences between Rae's theory and his own, Böhm-Bawerk concludes with the statement that in respect to one-half of his doctrine,—that, namely, which treats of the difference in the valuation of present and future goods and the importance of this phenomenon in the explanation of interest,—Rae deserves the credit of originality and of having anticipated him, but regarding the other half he declares that Rae was a follower of the productivity theorists, and especially of his great contemporary, Thünen.

The chapter on the exploitation theory has been considerably enlarged in the second edition by the addition of a section on "The Doctrines of Marx in the Mouths of his Successors," and by the extension of the critical portion of the section on Marx. The occasion of these additions was the publication in 1894 of the third volume of "Das Kapital," which existed only in manuscript at the time of the publication of the first edition and the contents of which were at that time unknown to the general public.

In the first two volumes many parts of Marx's theory were left incomplete, notably that portion of the doctrine of profits and of surplus value in which it became necessary to harmonize the law of the equalization of profits with the labour theory of value. Marx recognized two varieties of capital, which he distinguished by the terms "variable" and "constant." Variable capital is paid to labourers, and by means of their value-creating power reappears with a surplus. Constant capital reappears likewise, but without a surplus. It follows, therefore, that the rate of profits should be higher where the proportion of variable capital is large, and lower where it is small. The fact is, however, that the rate of profits tends toward equality without reference to the composition of the capital, and a consequence of this is that products do not exchange in accordance with the amounts of labour necessary to their production.

In his first volume Marx recognized the apparent discrepancy between his theory of value and the facts, and promised to harmonize the two in a subsequent publication, and the manuscript published in 1894 contained the fulfilment of that promise. Böhm-Bawerk shows, however, that he completely failed to remove this discrepancy. Marx's argument is that, though the law of the equalization of profits requires that the value of some goods should be too low and that of others too high, the excess of value in the one case exactly offsets the deficit in the other, and that, therefore, total values correspond to the amounts of labour which produced them. In criticism Böhm-

Bawerk shows that this argument completely overlooks the problem of value which is to explain the proportions in which goods exchange for each other, and not the relation between the sum of values and their labour costs. Marx's admission in the third volume, that goods actually do not exchange for each other in proportion to the amounts of labour necessary to their production, is a complete denial of the doctrine of value so elaborately worked out in the first volume. It is impossible to harmonize or to explain away so palpable a contradiction.

In Böhm-Bawerk's opinion the publication of the third volume of "Das Kapital" marks the beginning of the end of the labour theory of value. Some of Marx's followers of the present day have attempted to harmonize their master's contradictory statements, or at least to show that there is still a remnant of truth in the venerable theory, but our author finds little difficulty in exposing the futility of these attempts. The curious reader who does not understand German may examine these arguments and Böhm-Bawerk's criticisms in Miss

Macdonald's translation entitled "Karl Marx and the Close of his System."

Böhm-Bawerk's review of the literature of interest produced during the fifteen years preceding 1900, is presented herewith in translation, and needs no description or commendation. It speaks for itself. It is the hope and the belief of the translators that the English-speaking world will accord to this little book the same welcome they gave to the translation of the first edition.

WILLIAM A. SCOTT.

UNIVERSITY OF WISCONSIN,
May, 1903.

CONTENTS

RECENT LITERATURE ON INTEREST

CHAPTER I

INTRODUCTION

SINCE the appearance of the first edition of my work the problem of interest has been the subject of lively and varied discussions. The literature on this subject during the last fifteen years has been relatively more abundant than during any previous period of equal length, and while the strife which it indicates has brought no solution of the great problem, there is perceptible on the literary battle-field a certain shifting among the contending forces which seems to me to indicate a more advanced stage of the conflict, one approaching a final decision. The struggle is less desultory than it was fifteen years ago. Though some new opinions have appeared, many of the older ones have been entirely or almost entirely discarded, and the battle now centres about a few earnestly defended points between which the decision hangs. And even with reference to these the decision seems to me to be really nearer than ever before. There is no more skirmishing, no more fighting between advanced outposts. The preliminary actions have so far done their work, the premises and consequences of the contending theories, the essential nature of their theoretical content, so to speak, have been so clearly revealed, that the dispute can scarcely again deviate into side issues, and the pending decision must strike the very core of the matter.

To be the historian of the present is, for well-known reasons, a precarious matter. He who himself stands in the midst of the forest cannot easily obtain a good view of it. In my case there are two special reasons which render very difficult the task of being a good expositor of the present condition of the literature of interest. The fact that I myself am the author of one of the competing theories makes me partial in spite of the best of intentions, and, in particular, it is doubly difficult to preserve the right perspective in estimating the magnitude of the points at issue if to the nearness of the point of view be added the personal preference of the observer. Besides, the present generation of political economists are undoubtedly in the process of transforming their views regarding the interest problem. Whatever theory may finally maintain its ground, it is certain that the one which we shall transmit to the next generation as that of our times, will be essentially different from that which we found in the text-books of our youth and accepted as the basis of our thinking. We all, even the most conservative among us, have transformed the ideas which were transmitted to us. To review with an unbiassed historical eye and correctly to judge a literature in such a state of transformation, is a matter of peculiar and exceptional difficulty. One is confronted with a mass of transitional views, among which may be found, and apparently in the largest number, insignificant variations of expiring theories, as well as hopeful links in the chain of progressive development, and it would require an absolutely prophetic eye to decide with certainty whether a given theory is to be ranged in the one category or the other.

In spite of these difficulties, however, I should consider myself guilty of leaving a perceptible gap in the work which I have undertaken, if by these considerations I should permit myself to be frightened away from the task of attempting to give to my readers a critical survey of the contemporary literature of interest. Generally a critical history of doctrine is written for the purpose of illuminating the path of future investigation, and it would evidently on this account be in the highest degree improper if one were to leave in wilful darkness that portion of the road most recently covered and that point from which future travellers must start. However, I cannot proceed to this part of my task without the frankest acknowledgment of fallibility and insufficiency.

Regarding the larger part of the literature of the present day, I must limit myself in advance to a summary sketch. As a rule, I shall omit to present in detail and to discuss doctrines which are mere modifications of a main theory. And by so doing it is not my desire to indicate that I regard the modification as of little consequence or the respective doctrine as unimportant. I shall submit to an exhaustive exposition and criticism only a few of the most recent theories, indeed, only those which are either of such evident peculiarity that they are distinguished by essential characteristics from the types of theories previously described, or which, in case they are mere modifications or combinations of previous theories, have been so clearly formulated and at the same time so carefully worked out that the extent of the modification which they involve can be seen with perfect clearness.

CHAPTER II

THE AGIO THEORY

I HAVE already remarked that in the most recent times some new opinions have been added to the old rivals. The most influential additions of this sort are represented by those theories which explain interest by a difference in value between present and future goods.

Remote allusions to this thought had already been made by Galiani and Turgot. A half-century later John Rae had given to it a very remarkable formulation, in spite of which, however, it was not his fate to exert any influence upon its further literary development. Again, forty years later, Jevons worked out in a masterly way most of the premises upon which that theory rests, but he neglected to develop the lines of thought which connect these premises with the phenomena of interest. In this respect his work is inferior to that of his forgotten predecessor,

Rae, whom he about equals in the development of the psychological part of the premises and undoubtedly surpasses in the recognition of those premises which are derived from the technique of production.

In immediate connection with Jevons should be mentioned Launhardt[1] and Emil Sax.[2] Both of these authors excel Jevons in so far as they clearly express the concept, — involved, but not clearly expressed, in Jevons's work, and meantime announced in 1884 as the foundation of my interest theory, — that interest springs from the difference in value, resting upon psychological grounds, between present and future goods.[3] But

[1] "Mathematische Begründung der Volkswirtschaftlehre," Leipzig, 1885 (see especially pp. 5–7, 67 *sq.*, and 129).

[2] "Grundlegung der theoretischen Staatswirtschaft," Vienna, 1887 (pp. 178 *sq.*, 313 *sq.*).

[3] "The rate of interest demanded rests upon an estimation of the smaller value possessed by a future enjoyment in comparison with an equally great enjoyment offered in the present." (Launhardt, p. 129.)

"The value of a production good is derived from that of the consumption good which proceeds from it. Since the need which the production good indirectly satisfies is a future need, this derived value is smaller than that which the economic subject attributes to the consumption good available in the present

these authors merely formulated this principle without carrying it to its final consequences. Their failure to develop it in detail prevented them from testing whether the psychological causes of the lower estimation of future goods are able to furnish a sufficiently broad basis for a complete explanation of the phenomena of interest, or whether in addition certain facts connected with the technique of production, and entirely neglected by them, must not be employed in the explanation.

The works of Launhardt and Sax fall in the period between the appearance of the first (1884) and the second (1889) volumes of my published work upon "Capital and Interest." The "Positive Theory of Capital" set forth in the second volume contains an

for rendering the same satisfaction, or what amounts to the same thing, smaller than the value which that concrete consumption good, after it has come into existence, will have for him in view of the need which at that time exists. The value of the future consumption good from which the value of the capital is derived depends upon the future need, which is weaker than the need at present felt. . . . In the difference of value between the production good and the consumption good derived from it lies the so-called 'productivity' of capital." (Sax, pp. 317 and 321; cf. also p. 178 *sq.*)

attempt to derive all forms of the interest phenomenon from the difference in value between present and future goods, and to explain this difference by means of the coöperation of a series of causes, partly psychological and partly connected with the technique of production. This attempt met with much opposition, but also with agreement and support from many quarters. Cognate ideas were expressed at about the same time by American thinkers, especially by Simon N. Patten,[1] S. N. Macvane,[2] and J. B. Clark,[3] though in a less exhaustive way, and for the time being without any conscious break with the trend of ideas involved in the old abstinence theory.

1 "The Fundamental Idea of Capital," in the *Quarterly Journal of Economics*, January, 1889.

2 See his short but very noteworthy article entitled "Analysis of Cost of Production," in the *Quarterly Journal of Economics*, July, 1887, and later articles in the same periodical for October, 1890, and January, 1892.

3 The extensive series of articles in which this sagacious and indefatigable theorist has during the last decade presented his investigations on the subject of capital and interest begins with his monograph, "Capital and its Earnings," published in 1888. Most of his later articles may be found in the *Quarterly Journal of Economics*; some also in the *Annals of the American Academy*, July, 1890, and in the *Yale Review*, November, 1893.

At the same time there was in operation the impulse given by Jevons's brilliant work, which has steadily grown in the appreciation of the theorists of the various nations. The fact is that on account of one or the other of these stimulating influences, the theory of the difference in value between present and future goods, — to use a short expression, the agio theory,[1] — has taken root in the literature of all civilized nations, and has even acquired a predominant place in that of some of them. Especially it seems to me that cognate views, with this or that shade of difference, have acquired wide acceptance in English-American,[2] Italian,[3] Dutch,[4] and Scandinavian[5] literature.[6]

[1] Macfarlane ("Value and Distribution," pp. xxii and 230 *sq.*) proposes the name "exchange theory," because according to this theory interest arises from an exchange between present and future goods. But this term does not seem to me to characterize the theory sufficiently. By a strange misunderstanding, Zaleski ("Lehre vom Capital," Kazan, 1898) regards the title "Positive Theory of Capital," which I gave to the second part of my work in order to contrast it with the historical first part, as a characteristic attribute of my theory.

[2] Besides the authors included in the text there are others who hold more or less similar views. For example, J. Bonar (*Quarterly Journal of Economics*, April and October, 1889, and April,

1890); William Smart ("Introduction to the Theory of Value," London, 1891, "The New Theory of Interest," *Economic Journal*, 1891); F. Y. Edgeworth (*Economic Journal*, June, 1892); E. B. Andrews ("Institutes of Economics," Boston, 1889); Lowrey (*Annals of American Academy*, March, 1892); Ely ("Outlines of Economics," New York, 1893); Carver (*Quarterly Journal of Economics*, October, 1893); Taussig ("Wages and Capital," New York, 1896); Irving Fisher (*Economic Journal*, December, 1896, June and December, 1897); Mixter ("A Forerunner of Böhm-Bawerk," *Quarterly Journal of Economics*, January, 1897); Macfarlane ("Value and Distribution," Philadelphia, 1899); and especially also Hobson ("Evolution of Modern Capitalism," London, 1894); and Hadley ("Economics," New York, 1896, and *Annals of American Academy*, November, 1893). Giddings has also expressed himself as partially in agreement with this idea, but he believes that in order to complete and extend the theory, it is necessary to make an addition to it, in which he would explain the constant deficiency in the supply of present goods or capital by the fact that the last hours of labour, performed with ever increasing reluctance and pain, contribute to the formation of capital. This increase in the pains of labour constitutes the extra costs of capital building, — in comparison with the cost of the manufacture of goods designed for immediate consumption — which extra costs must find their remuneration in interest. But I am neither able to convince myself of the reality of all the assumptions of fact involved in this theory, nor, if these assumptions be granted, am I able to discover their operation in the process by which interest is produced. See, besides, the exhaustive discussion in the *Quarterly Journal of Economics* from July, 1889, to April, 1891, in which, besides Giddings and myself, Bonar, David J. Green, and H. Bilgram also took part.

[3] Ricca-Salerno ("Teorie del Valore," Rome, 1894), Montemartini ("Il Risparmio dell' Economia pura," Milan, 1896); Crocini ("Di alcune questioni relative all' utilità finale," Turin, 1896); Graziani ("Studi sulla teoria dell' interesse," Turin, 1898); further

in essentials perhaps, Barone ("Sopra un libro di Wicksell," *Giornale degli Economisti*, November, 1895, and "Studi sulla distributione" in the same journal for February and March, 1896); and partly at least, Benini ("Il valore e la sua attribuzione ai beni strumentali," Bari, 1893).

[4] Under this head must be mentioned before all others N. G. Pierson's classical work, "Leerboek der Staatshuishoudkunde" (2d ed., Harlem, 1896, and an older article in *De Economist*, March, 1899, p. 193 *sq.*).

[5] This subject has been most exhaustively treated by Kunt Wicksell ("Ueber Wert, Capital und Rent," Jena, 1893, "Finanztheoretische Untersuchungen," Jena, 1896). Dr. Wicksell was kind enough to supplement my insufficient knowledge of Scandinavian literature by some private communications, in which he mentions as representatives of cognate views the following authors: in Denmark, Professors Westergaard and Folbe-Hansen; in Sweden, Count Hamilton, David Davidson, and John Leffler; in Norway, Professors Aschehoug and Morgenstierne, Dr. Oskar Jäeger and Dr. Einarsen.

[6] Among the original German works in which similar ideas are expressed, I wish to make special mention of that of Effertz ("Arbeit und Boden," Berlin, 1889), which appeared almost contemporaneously with my "Positive Theory," and the profound work of the Swiss author, George Sulzer ("Die wirtschaftlichen Grundgesetze in der Gegenwartsphase ihrer Entwicklung," Zurich, 1895). Effertz expressed in an original way the thought that interest owes its existence to a difference of time, and that the "age" ("alter") of labour and of land is an element of exchange value, and that interest is "the payment for the age quality of labour and land" (pp. 190 *sq.*, 198 *sq.*, and 278). The necessity of the additional payment for the "age" of the elements of production is remotely, although perhaps inadequately, explained by the fact that old labour and old land are rarer than present labour and present land (pp. 190, 195, 198; cf. also in addition, pp. 218, 221, 354). The fact that the author on principle avoids literary

references makes it impossible to know whether and to what extent the work of Effertz, which appeared in 1889, was influenced by several previous discussions of the same fundamental thought. Sulzer's treatment of the subject seems to me in general to move upon a middle line between that of Jevons and my own. On the position occupied by Adolf Wagner at the present time, see Chapter V.

CHAPTER III

THE USE THEORIES

Of the numerous opinions which have contended for mastery upon the literary battlefields of the past, some have received no reënforcement whatever in recent times, and others have had only an occasional champion. Of the first kind, for the most part, has been the fate of those groups of theories which have either reduced the problem of interest to too great simplicity, or have subjected it to a refinement of treatment which is fatal. For the first reason the colourless theories,[1] the naive productivity theory, the fructification theory

[1] I am almost inclined to class under this head the interest theory of Lehr ("Grundbegriffe und Grundlagen der Volkswirtschaft," Leipzig, 1893, Pt. VII, Ch. 6); at least, I am unable to discover any characteristic point in his rather voluminous disquisition upon this subject. He refuses his adherence to most of the theories ordinarily held, but on his part presents only such statements as in substance constitute either an appeal to the reality, propriety, justice, and equity of certain phenomena or echo certain universal motives (such as the motive referred to by Adam Smith, that without the prospect of interest, capital would

of Turgot, and the theory of Henry George, have remained without new adherents; and for the second reason theories of the type of Schellwien's.

To the group which has only received occasional reënforcement belongs the interesting use theory. From its most distinguished representative, Karl Menger, nothing new has appeared; though in his highly esteemed monograph on "The Theory of Capital"[1] this author has subjected the concept of capital to a thoroughgoing and fruitful investigation, which, however, does not extend to the contested question of interest. Walras, who had previously expounded the use theory in a form which reminds us of J. B. Say, still holds to this theory.[2]

Among recent works which adhere clearly

not be accumulated for purposes of production or loan, p. 332), but in my opinion constitute no real explanation of the phenomenon of interest.

[1] Conrad's *Jahrbücher*, new series, Vol. XXII (1888).

[2] "Eléments d'Économie politique pure," 1st ed., Lausanne, 1874, 2d ed., 1889. Walras considers interest as the payment for the productive service ("service producteur") of capital, which is a distinct immaterial good (see, for example, pp. 201, 211, and XIII of the 2d ed.). In essentials Pareto (Cours d'Économie

and firmly to the standpoint of the use theory (occasional allusions to this theory are frequent, especially among eclectic writers[1]), only that of Ladislas Zaleski in the Russian language on "The Doctrine of Capital"[2] is known to me. Since for linguistic reasons my knowledge of this work is confined to a few extracts placed at my disposal, I can only make the statement that Zaleski expresses his adherence to the use theory and attempts to base it upon the doctrine of natural science regarding "the unity of matter and the conservation of energy." How far removed he is in this new departure from the use theory of Menger, and to what extent he approaches the intricate productivity theory, I am unable to say.

politique, Vol. I, p. 40 *sq.*) adheres to the conception of Walras, but not without occasional allusions to the difference in value between present and future goods (see, for example, p. 50).

[1] For example, Conrad ("Grundriss zum Studium der politischen Ökonomie," Jena, 1896, Pt. I, § 67); Dietzel, in an article quoted farther on (*Göttinger gelehrten Anzeigen*); Diehl ("Proudhon, seine Lehre und sein Leben," Jena, 1890, Pt. II, p. 204); M. Block ("Progrès de la science Économique depuis Adam Smith," Paris, 1890, Pt. II, Ch. XXIX); Ch. Gide ("Principes d'Économie Politique," 5th ed., Paris, 1896, p. 451); and several others.

[2] Kazan, 1898.

CHAPTER IV

THE ABSTINENCE THEORY

DURING the last fifteen years the abstinence theory has been the subject of lively, I may almost say unexpectedly lively, theoretical discussion. To begin with some details, it has received support of an interesting kind from the fact that it has been vigorously defended by some writers against an objection which has played a very noisy part in the polemic directed against it by socialistic agitators. The objection is that the greatest capitalists have occasion to practise the least abstinence, and that therefore there is an evident lack of harmony between the magnitude of the causes which are supposed to be in operation, that is, the abstinence practised, and their supposed effect, the amount of interest obtained.

By the application of a principle common to the Ricardian and the marginal utility theories, it has been shown that this lack of harmony cannot be regarded as a conclusive argument against the truth of the abstinence theory, since the market price of products by which the sacrifice involved in their production is remunerated tends to equal the greatest of the various sacrifices required. On this account it is not remarkable that the same rate of interest which is adequate to reward the greatest abstinence undergone may give an excessive remuneration to those persons with whom the accumulation and maintenance of capital involves a relatively small sacrifice of abstinence.[1] But this argument answers only one of the most superficial objections to the abstinence theory, and does not touch the more funda-

[1] In his apology for the abstinence theory, Macfarlane ("Value and Distribution," Philadelphia, 1899, pp. 175–177) lays the strongest emphasis upon this line of thought. Substantially in agreement with him are Loria ("La Rendita Fondiaria," Milan, 1880, p. 619 *sq.*), and Marshall with his theory of "saver's surplus" ("Principles," 3d ed., London, 1895, p. 606); see further Carver, Barone, and indeed in general all investigators who recognize the marginal utility theory of value and who at the same time are inclined to adhere to the abstinence theory; see also p. 277 *sq.* of Smart's translation of "Capital and Interest."

mental one, based on logical grounds, upon which I have constructed my criticism of it.[1]

A significant change in terminology has been suggested by Macvane, who proposes to substitute for the expression "abstinence," which has been the occasion of so much opposition, the weaker but more suitable term "waiting."[2] This suggestion involves a certain approach to the standpoint of that theory which in the explanation of interest lays chief stress upon the influence of the element of time upon the difference in value between present and future enjoyments and goods, and it is a significant fact that not a few of the most recent representatives of the abstinence theory regard this and the agio theory as substantially identical.[3] But there is a real ob-

[1] A remark of Macfarlane's (p. 179) bearing upon my objection does not appear to me to strike the heart of the matter, but to consist of a mere counter-proposition.

[2] "Analysis of Cost of Production" (*Quarterly Journal of Economics*, July, 1887). See also above, p. 9.

[3] For example, Macfarlane is of the opinion that the "exchange theory," as he calls it (see also above, p. 10, note 1), of the essential features of which he approves, is only an improved and developed form of the theory of Böhm-Bawerk ("the theory here proposed is after all but an extension of Böhm-Bawerk's

stacle in the way of the amalgamation of these two theories, namely, that to the "waiting," which Macvane and his followers suggest as a milder term than abstinence, must be assigned the position of an independent sacrifice which must be paid for in addition to that of labour.

The inclination of the abstinence theorists, which was noticeable in previous periods, to introduce in an eclectic way into their discussions of the interest problem propositions which belong to other types of theories, is also perceptible in the most recent times. Similar to the incorporation of elements of the agio theory, which has just been described, is another combination with elements of the exploitation theory,[1] for which Loria is responsible.

analysis." "Value and Distribution," p. 231). For this improved form he also suggests the improved title "normal value theory." Carver holds a similar opinion regarding the relation between the two theories (see below), and perhaps also Professor Marshall.

[1] I do not believe that I am in error in assigning the ideas of Loria, which in all respects are not perfectly clear to me, in the main to the abstinence theory. At least the clearest passages in his older works ("Rendita Fondiaria," p. 610 *sq.*, and "Analisi della Proprietà Capitalista," Turin, 1889) point in this direction, and in agreement therewith is the idea expressed in the most recent comprehensive work of the author ("La Costituzione

Out of this group of theories, two must be selected for special treatment, one because it is a model exposition of a completely developed, up-to-date abstinence theory, backed by the authority of one of the most distinguished scholars. Endowed with all the gifts essential to an investigator and expositor, Alfred Marshall has furnished us a complete explanation of interest comprehending all the facts which have a bearing upon the question. The

economica odierna," Turin, 1899), namely, that the abstinence of capitalists must be regarded as an element which plays an essential rôle in the distribution of the product (see, for example, pp. 36 *sq.* and 75). In the same direction also point the expressions of the author regarding the motive and limits of accumulation (for example, "Costituzione," pp. 73 *sq.* and 98 *sq.*). Still, in the works of Loria may be found also expressions which warrant one in concluding that in this author's opinion the fact of exploitation has an important part in the phenomenon of interest, at least in its present form and extent (for example, "Costituzione," pp. 34 *sq.* and 821). A well-known specialty of Loria's is the doctrine that to the appropriation of land is to be ascribed a decisive and far-reaching influence upon the formation and magnitude of the profits of capital. I regard this opinion as entirely wrong (a more complete exposition and criticism of this may be found in Graziani's brilliant "Studi sulla teoria dell' interesse," Turin, 1898, pp. 46–50), and I cannot suppress the remark that to me the theoretical speculations of Loria appear much more fantastic than exact, and seem to me frequently to be permeated by very superficial misunderstandings of the opinions of others.

second of these theories deserves attention as an original attempt to give an entirely new meaning to the term "sacrifice of abstinence."

Professor Marshall recognizes the fundamental causes of interest in two circumstances which he describes by the terms, the "prospectiveness" and the "productiveness" of capital. The "prospectiveness" of capital consists in the fact that it yields its uses (nützen) only in the future. In order to accumulate capital, people must act prospectively; they must wait and save; they must sacrifice the present to the future.[1] "Productiveness" is based upon the productive advantages which the assistance of capital furnishes. It makes production easier and more abundant.[2] The "produc-

[1] "Principles of Economics," 3d ed., pp. 142, 662. The fourth edition, which has appeared in the meantime, is in all essentials in agreement with the third.

[2] pp. 142, 622, 751. In this, and in general in all passages in which Professor Marshall explains "productiveness," he very properly has in mind a technical productivity which shows itself in an addition to the product which could be obtained with the same expenditure of original productive powers. He is, therefore, in entire agreement with the conception of physical or technical productivity which I have employed in my theory of interest. It appears that Professor Marshall is also in agreement with me in that he regards capitalistic production as production

tivity" of capital makes it an object of demand, but on account of the sacrifice connected with its productiveness, the supply is kept at so low a point that the use of capital brings a price and becomes a source of profit.[1]

Further particulars regarding this proposition result from the universal law of exchange, of which Marshall regards interest as merely a special case. According to that universal law, the "normal" value of commodities tends constantly to adjust itself to that level at which demand is in equilibrium with the cost of production. Marshall lays special emphasis upon the coördinate position of these two factors which mutually influence each other. The real costs of production are made up of the totality of exertions and sacrifices which must be undergone in the production of goods. Besides labour these include also the sacrifice of waiting or of the postponement of enjoyment which is inseparably connected with the accumulation and employment of capital.[2]

by roundabout methods (cf. "Principles," p. 612, and also the note on p. 664, which indicates a dissenting view).

[1] p. 662.

[2] pp. 216, 315.

The term "abstinence," which has been widely used since the days of the older economists, Marshall regards as less suitable than waiting, and as the fruitful source of misunderstandings, since the largest accumulations of capital are made by very rich people who experience no abstinence in the sense of privation. It would, therefore, be more correct if, following Macvane's example, we should designate the content of the sacrifice under consideration as a mere postponement of enjoyment. This, however, constitutes a real sacrifice which must be reckoned separately, and in addition to that of labour (p. 668).

Like the sacrifice of labour this one must find its compensation in the average price of commodities according to their marginal rate (p. 607); that is, the payment must be large enough adequately to remunerate even the most unpleasant and the most repulsive part of the sacrifice necessarily put forth in the production of the necessary supply (p. 217). This payment is interest, and is, therefore, fittingly described as the reward of the sacrifice involved in waiting (p. 314). To be sure, many people would save without such a reward, just as many people would work without any wage. Therefore, a considerable capital would be accumulated, even with a lower interest rate than that which controls the market. From this it follows that on account of the general principle that the price must adequately remunerate the greatest sacrifice involved in the production of the supply, the savers of this capital receive a remuneration in excess of the lesser sacrifice which they undergo, a remuneration which Marshall designates as "saver's" or "waiter's surplus." But since few people would make any considerable accumulations of capital without the remuneration involved in interest, it is likewise proper to explain interest as the "reward of waiting" (p. 314). In reply to the socialists who maintain that the value of goods depends simply upon the quantity of labour expended in their production, Marshall maintains with emphasis that the view of the socialists would be correct only on condition that the service rendered by capital be offered as a free good without sacrifice, but that it is incorrect in case the postponement of gratification involves in general a sacrifice on the part of him who postpones (p. 668).

I do not think I am wrong in designating the view held by Marshall as in essentials a cautiously formulated abstinence theory with an improved terminology. In its fundamentals his doctrine is in complete agreement with that of Senior. The formation of capital demands on the part of capitalists a real sacrifice which consists in the postponement of enjoyment and forms an independent element in the cost of production side by side with labour. For this an independent payment must be found in the price of goods after the manner and according to the laws (to be sure, more carefully formulated by Marshall) by which in general costs influence the price of goods.[1] Under these circumstances it is evident that my view of Professor Marshall's interest theory cannot differ much from that which I expressed regarding the abstinence theory in general in my book on "Capital and

[1] Cf. the exposition of Senior's theory to be found in my "Capital and Interest," Smart's translation, p. 271 *sq*.

Interest." Though I am in full agreement with him on the point that the "prospectiveness" as well as the "productiveness" of capital have something to do with the explanation of interest, I think that the explanation by which he and other abstinence theorists connect these phenomena with interest, is presented in a form which is not in harmony with the facts and which is in unavoidable conflict with the laws of thought.

In the first place, I regard as incorrect the contention that in the act of postponement which is involved in the employment of labour for the acquisition of a pleasure to be experienced at a remote period of time, we must recognize a separate sacrifice to be reckoned independent of and in addition to that of labour. The grounds[1] for this opinion I have already presented in an exhaustive manner. However, if Professor Marshall, well acquainted with them as he is, still holds fast to his doctrine, which is in essentials identical with the abstinence theory, they do not appear to have been sufficiently convincing. I will, therefore,

[1] Smart's translation, Bk. IV.

endeavour to support them by some further explanations, and for this a welcome opportunity is presented to me by some remarks which may be found in Professor Marshall's exposition of his theory.

Like Jevons,[1] Marshall has included in his theory some psychological elements regarding the estimation of future pains and pleasures. Human nature is actually so formed that most men do not esteem a future pleasure, even though its acquisition is absolutely certain, so highly as a present pleasure of the same sort, but they discount it or make a deduction from it, the magnitude of which varies with different people according to the varying degrees of their patience and self-control.[2] The present

[1] See Smart's translation, p. 403 *sq.*

[2] "Principles," pp. 195–197, 794, *et passim.* In this connection Marshall distinguishes as clearly as is necessary the under-estimation of future pleasures from other differences in valuation, which may proceed from a difference in time, but arise from another source. Such, on the one hand, are the lower estimates of future pleasures and goods which spring from the insecurity of their acquisition, and, on the other hand, differences in valuation which arise from the fact that by a change in other circumstances the character or the magnitude of the future pleasure is itself changed. For example, by a prospective change in the capacity

value of future pleasures, and, therefore, also the present marginal utility of a distant source of pleasure, are, therefore, smaller than the value of a like present pleasure or even than the value of the same future pleasure at the time when it actually appears. If, for example, according to his temperament, some one is accustomed to discount future pleasures at the rate of ten per cent, he will to-day esteem at ten the present worth of a pleasure which is still one year distant, and which will then have, roughly estimated,[1] an actual value of eleven. From numerous remarks of Marshall, it appears that the psychological fact that the great mass of mankind gives to present satisfactions the preference over future is precisely the one upon which he founds his claim that waiting involves a sacrifice.[2] That in general we give

for enjoyment (an Alpine tour at an advanced age), or by a change in the abundance of the supply which exerts an influence upon a final utility (eggs which are saved for the winter).

[1] That is, with the omission of compound interest. Marshall himself develops for this an accurate algebraic formula in note 5 of the appendix to his "Principles."

[2] pp. 313 *sq.*, 429, n. 1, 662, 663, n. 1, and 668; indirectly also, p. 794, n. 5, in so far as interest, which elsewhere he explains as

present pleasures the preference over equally great future ones, and that in general we feel that waiting for a future enjoyment is a sacrifice which increases the expense of acquisition, are in Marshall's doctrine only two different methods of expression for one and the same psychological fact. As a matter of fact, however, they are not only different modes of expression, but different modes of conception, and, indeed, — a fact which is of interest for our purpose, — two discordant and incompatible modes of conception, of which the one is right and the other wrong, and which it is impossible to hold at the same time, and side by side with each other. The fact of the matter is as follows: —

It is a common experience, doubted by no one, that the psychological phenomenon whose real meaning is now in question reveals itself in the fact, among others, that for gratifications equal in all respects except in their remoteness from us in time we are inclined to undergo unequally great sacrifices of labour or money. For

"the reward of waiting," is brought into connection with the "discounting" of future pleasures.

example, if the amount of the gratification be ten, we will be inclined to devote to its acquisition a labour sacrifice up to the amount ten or an equivalent sacrifice in money, say up to ten florins, if this gratification be attainable at the moment. If, on the other hand, the same gratification be removed from us one year, and if the psychological fact in our special case acts with a force corresponding to a discount rate of ten per cent, we will be inclined to expend upon its acquisition a present amount of labour of, at the most, something more than nine (accurately 9.09) or a money sacrifice of, in the aggregate, something more than nine florins (9 fl. 9 kr.). If the same gratification stood five years distant, our willingness to acquire the same through a present sacrifice of labour or money would find its limits in about six units (accurately 6.21) of labour-pain or about 6 fl. 21 kr. of money.[1]

This fact, regarding the reality of which, as I have already said, there is no difference of

[1] For simplicity's sake, in this and the following cases I assume that the entire sacrifice of labour or money is made at once; that is, at one, and that the present, point of time.

opinion between Marshall and myself,[1] admits of two explanations. One is that the distance of the gratification from us in time diminishes, in our eyes, its magnitude. Because it is future, we place a lower estimate upon a utility than we would if it were present. It is this explanation which finds expression in the remarks of Marshall mentioned above regarding the estimation of future pleasures. The present value of a future pleasure is less than ten; when removed from us one year it is only about nine, when removed from us five years, only about six; and because the gratification is worth no more to us than nine and six respectively, we are unwilling, for its acquisition, to submit to any greater sacrifice than is indicated by the figures 9 and 6.

It is now evident that, according to this conception, the figures 9 and 6 must indicate and limit not merely the magnitude of a part of

[1] Marshall illustrates this, for example, in the case of the building of a house, the utility of which when finished must cover the efforts required for building in addition to an amount, increasing in geometrical proportions (a sort of compound interest) for the period which would elapse between each effort and the time when the house would be ready for use (p. 429).

the sacrifice of labour and money, but the magnitude of the whole sacrifice which we are inclined to take upon ourselves for the acquisition of a future enjoyment. In other words, according to this explanation there is no room for a sacrifice of "waiting" in addition to that of labour or money, for it is evident that it would be opposed to all the principles of economic action that for a pleasure which we esteemed at only 9 or 6 we should be willing to undergo an amount of sacrifice consisting of labour and waiting, or of money and waiting, in excess of the value of the gratification itself; for example, an amount equal to ten.

The second conceivable explanation leads to the same result. We met this one in the expressions of Marshall regarding the existence of a sacrifice of waiting which must be separately reckoned in addition to and by the side of that of labour. In this instance the facts of the case are explained in the following manner: The prospect of the future gratification which after one or five years shall have a value of ten causes us to take upon ourselves an amount of sacrifice consisting of labour and waiting, which, in view of the degree of painfulness and the supposed continuance of the waiting, is estimated at ten.

It is again evident, I believe, that this explanation of the facts presupposes that the prospect of the gratification to be acquired in the future operates upon our present calculations with the full undiminished magnitude of that gratification. But, if we estimate the future gratification at its undiminished magnitude of ten, we cannot, acting intelligently and economically, decide to take upon ourselves for its acquisition a total sacrifice of the magnitude of ten. The abstinence theory, however, lays especial emphasis upon this thought. It teaches that the value of a future production or consumption good cannot be brought to a lower level than ten (to speak again in terms of our example), because the addition of the sacrifice of waiting raises the amount of the total cost to that sum, and the producer would not consider himself sufficiently remunerated for this sacrifice if the commodity brought a lower price. This process of reasoning expressly presupposes that the value of the future commodity figures in the calculations of the producer with an undiminished magnitude of ten.

In other words, it is evident that we can only employ the second of these explanations if we turn our backs upon the first. We must hold either that the postponement of the gratification expected in the future diminishes its utility in our estimation, or that it increases in our estimation the sacrifice to be undergone by the amount of the waiting; but we cannot hold to both explanations at the same time. It would be economic and mathematical nonsense to hold that, if in the calculations of the producer the future utility should fall from ten to six, while the sacrifice on account of the addition of the element due to waiting should at the same time be increased from six to ten, the production would be found remunerative.[1]

[1] In order to forestall every possible misunderstanding, I will at once meet a certain objection which may possibly be urged. A superficial observer may, perhaps, be tempted to explain the matter in the following manner. The future utility of ten, to be acquired only after five years, will, in fact, in our present estimation, be perspectively diminished, and thus estimated at only

If, then, one must choose between the two conceptions which Professor Marshall has

6.21, and over against this present value of the gratification stands a present sacrifice in labour or money of 6.21. The sacrifice of waiting, on the other hand, appears first in the future, and will find its compensation in the then full future value of the gratification, in amount, ten. On the one hand, therefore, present value and present sacrifice offset each other, and on the other, the future value is in harmony with the total magnitude of sacrifice, which includes also that of the future. In this process of thought, however, the fact is overlooked that every rational economic calculation must include the sacrifices not yet due as well as those at present experienced. If I propose to myself the problem, whether I shall buy a dwelling house offered me for the payment of twenty annual instalments of 1000 florins each, I may not bring the present value of the house into comparison with the rate of sacrifice at present experienced, that is, with the first instalment of 1000 florins alone, but I must, of course, place over against the value of the house the value of the entire twenty instalments. To be sure, the instalments not yet due will enter the calculation at their reduced present value. In an analogous manner, and according to the abstinence theory, the total sacrifice which must be made for a remote gratification consists of present sacrifice of labour or money, and of a series of further sacrifices of waiting spread over the entire period of time. In our present calculations this latter, like the instalments on the house due at a later period, may enter into the account only after the deduction of a certain discount corresponding to the distance of their removal from us in time. But they must certainly, in some way, be taken into consideration, especially since, as we know, in the case of the abstinence theorists, it is precisely the consideration of these which should hold the producers back from directing production toward less valuable future goals. In our illustration, this conception would be expressed in the fol-

brought together in his theory, the choice cannot be doubtful, I think, even to the distinguished scientist whose opinion I am compelled to oppose. On the one side the experience that people, and even careless people, rate the prospect of a future gratification lower than a present gratification of the same magnitude is very much too pronounced

lowing manner: The labour or money sacrifice to be endured amounts to 6.21; the sum of the sacrifices of five years of waiting, through which the total sacrifice is brought up to 10, amounts accordingly to 3.79. Since, however, these sacrifices of waiting belong still to the future, and indeed are to be experienced on the average only after two and a half years, their present value is estimated correspondingly lower; that is, on the basis of a discount rate of 10 per cent, at about 2.96. According to this the present value of the sacrifices to be considered would amount to $6.21 + 2.96 = 9.17$. The present value of the gratification to be obtained, however, amounts to only 6.21. The proportion between these aggregates, therefore, precludes any intelligent economic action.

Frankly speaking, I am astonished that Professor Marshall has not felt disturbed in his mathematical treatment of the whole question by such unavoidable numerical incongruities. To be sure, I myself am too little of a mathematician to be able to decide how and why it has been possible for Professor Marshall to conceal from himself or to veil such real and unquestioned errors in the mathematical tables developed by him in which he expresses the progressive diminution in the value of future gratifications as well as the progressive increase of the sacrifice of waiting. (Notes 13 and 14 of his mathematical Appendix.)

to permit of denial, and on the other side those objections which count against the existence of an independent sacrifice of abstinence or of waiting, and which I have worked out in detail in the ninth chapter of my book, will gain in weight, on account of the necessity of a choice, even in the eyes of those who have up to this time been unimpressed by them. I believe that upon a renewed and careful investigation of the question, the conviction can scarcely be avoided in the long run that non-enjoyment is not suffering, and that an unfruitful piece of work cannot be represented by a limited quantity of labour sacrifice and by an unlimited quantity of sacrifice composed of waiting to all eternity. However, in case that in the minds of especially sceptical readers some remnant of doubt should still remain, I wish in conclusion to submit also the following considerations:—

He who, according to the meaning of the abstinence theorists, regards waiting as an independent sacrifice, must be content with the deduction that even careless persons who take no thought for the future are inclined to make an equally great sacrifice for the acquisition of an enjoyment never so far removed as for one which entices them at the moment. The equally great sums of sacrifice are only made up in different ways; in the case of present gratifications, out of work alone; in the case of future gratifications, out of somewhat less work and an amount of waiting sufficient to bring the total sacrifice up to the same level.

Still further, without any doubt, and even according to Marshall, the psychological phenomenon here under discussion is extended not only to the valuation of future pleasures, but also to that of future pains. Let us suppose that some one is threatened by an ill which, if precautions are not now taken, will come upon him one year hence, and at that time will have a magnitude represented by ten. Certain it is that this person, if he discounts future events at the rate of ten per cent, will not be inclined to undergo a sacrifice represented by a greater figure than 9 for the purpose of warding off that ill. Now, on a pinch, I can conceive that if the preparation in question concerns some sort of positive gratification, the waiting for that gratification might be felt as a sacrifice, which would swell the total sacrifice successively up to ten, but I cannot possibly imagine what sacrifice is involved in my inability to remove a threatened ill which does not yet press upon me. What "painful endurance of want" lies in the fact that in midsummer I am not in possession of the overcoat in process of preparation on the spindles and looms; or in the fact that a young man of thirty, who at the age of fifty expects to need a pair of glasses for long-sightedness, must wait twenty years for the preparation of those glasses, for the production of which meantime remote preparatory labours in mine and factory have already been begun? To the unprejudiced observer I believe that the connection is as clear as daylight. By a painful waiting for the removal of an evil not yet present the sacrifice side of the scales is not more and more weighed down until it is equal to the full magnitude of a utility of ten, but the balance of both sides of the scales was established in the beginning at the moment, alone decisive, in which the economic calculation and decision was made, and by the fact that the estimation of the threatening future ill was perspectively diminished, and that its removal was therefore looked upon as a correspondingly smaller utility, and that in consequence a sacrifice of labour of correspondingly lesser magnitude would be regarded as its equivalent.[1]

[1] If some one should here object that the labour which is expended as a precaution against the future pain might have been expended also in the preparation of a present positive gratification, and that the loss of this other gratification forms the content of the sacrifice of waiting, I should think first of all that by such a method of viewing the situation the fundamental question was only avoided, not solved, and in the second place I should propose that such a method of eluding the question be cut off by considering a concrete situation. Let us assume, for instance, that the subject of our example is a prisoner who has no winter clothing, and who knows that his dismissal will occur in the course of a year, and at the time of the greatest cold of winter, and who, according to the regulations of the prison, is permitted, but not compelled, to earn a sum sufficient to purchase winter clothes by labour which he is not permitted to employ in any other way, or for the securing of any earlier gratifications during the continuance of his incarceration. In this case there is absolutely no room for the sacrifice of waiting in addition to that of labour which would be imposed upon him by the devotion of his labour to the acquisition of warm winter clothes, and he

The fundamental error of the abstinence theory, therefore, consists in the fact that it puts on the wrong side of the balance those differences which are undoubtedly created by the remoteness of time, and which exert an unfavourable influence upon the balance of our welfare; that it sees a greater sacrifice, where in reality there is a diminution in utility, and that thus it makes a wrong choice between the two conceivable interpretations of the facts. Professor Marshall, however, and with him all those scientists[1] who have considered the psychological fact, introduced into the science by Rae and Jevons, of the smaller estimation of future pleasures and pains as identical with the recognition of the abstinence theory, makes an additional error, in that he fails ut-

who does not entirely deny the fact that even in the case of a man who finds himself in this condition the regard for the future can be less efficient than that for the present will indeed be forced to declare the second interpretation, recommended also by so many other considerations, as the only one permissible, namely, that the remoteness in time diminishes the magnitude of future pleasures and pains in our present estimation.

[1] As, for example, in former times John Stuart Mill and Jevons, in our day Macfarlane, and indeed also Carver; in reference to the last see farther on.

terly to see that a choice must here be made between two conceptions which cannot possibly exist side by side.

This is the most important, but not the only reason why I am unable to regard Professor Marshall's treatment of the interest problem as a satisfactory solution. As I have had occasion to remark in another place,[1] Professor Marshall is inclined to lay very little stress upon mere differences, or imperfections in the method of expressing a thought, and at the same time is inclined to regard very important differences as mere variations in the form of expression. There can be no doubt, however, that we are not here concerned with merely a less commendable form of expressing a correct thought. We are concerned with an essential and characteristic link in a logical chain of thought which should result in an explanation of interest. That Professor Marshall, himself, regards this critical link as a very essential one, is evident from the fact that he, although, as I think, wrongly, makes the entire decision between his conception and

[1] See my Preface to the second edition.

that of the socialists hang upon the question whether waiting is to be construed as an independent sacrifice in addition to that of labour or not.[1] That, in any case, there is a material difference between his view of the matter and mine becomes clear from the fact that, according to his conception, the disappearance of that psychological fact which expresses itself in the preference of present for future goods must also have as its result the disappearance of interest,[2] while, according to my opinion, in

[1] p. 668 *sq*.

[2] Marshall himself regards such a change in our physical and moral disposition as by no means inconceivable, and as a logical result of his explanation of interest as a reward for the sacrifice involved in waiting, he gives us clearly to understand that it is his opinion that in such a case "interest would be negative all along the line." To be sure, he expects this result also in the case in which, without a complete disappearance of all preference for equally great present enjoyments, the care for old age and family has become so strong in so many people that the sums saved for this purpose are more than adequate for the new openings for the advantageous use of accumulated wealth (p. 663, n. 1). For subtle investigators I may add that by this last clause, referring to advantageous opportunities for production, a complete material agreement of our opinions has not been established, for on the one hand, in my opinion, even in a completely stationary state, and even if opportunities for new investments of capital were entirely wanting, the superior productivity of the roundabout process of production would be sufficient to main-

that case only one of several sources of the interest phenomena would be dried up. In-

tain interest for any length of time (on this point see especially my monograph on "Some Controverted Questions in the Theory of Interest," Vienna, 1900); and on the other hand, in the passage cited, Professor Marshall apparently regards the frequent appearance of new opportunities for the investment of capital as an obstacle to the complete disappearance of interest only on condition that some difference of estimation between present and future enjoyments otherwise equal still persists. As Professor Marshall has himself explained with unrivalled clearness (p. 197, n. 1), a distinction must be drawn between enjoyments and goods as objects of a different valuation with regard to the present and the future. In the case of goods a very influential rôle can be played by the circumstance that the same sum yields unequally great objective marginal utilities in different periods of time. Therefore, a person who in and for himself would prefer a present enjoyment to an equally great future one, may nevertheless decide to save, even without the prospect of an increase in interest in case the sum saved and to be transferred to the future, that is, to the point of time of a needy old age, yields at that time a correspondingly greater marginal utility than it would have yielded in case of its consumption at the moment. Evidently Professor Marshall's argument has reference to this consideration. So long as the need for new investments of capital is met by the saving of those among whom the underestimation of future pleasures is compensated by the increase of the objective marginal utility of the sums of goods transferred to the future, no sacrifice of abstinence needed for such remuneration appears, and interest may be wanting. However, if the amount of capital needed for new investments exceeds this sum, then the underestimation of future enjoyments will not be covered by the increase in the objective utilities of like quantities of goods, and terest itself would continue, though with diminished strength, because, even without any underestimation of the future, the fact that more roundabout methods of production are more fruitful must secure[1] to present goods which render possible the undertaking of such roundabout processes a superiority of value over future goods, not merely for the moment, but for periods of time, which, measured by the strictest standard, must be counted as the longest "secular" periods.[2]

In conclusion, I wish to remark that in Marshall may be found still another class of expressions in which he has established a special connection between interest and the use of capital, and which, if they were the only ones

must therefore be remunerated by interest. If this be the real opinion of Professor Marshall, and I doubt not that it is, then in his mind the continued existence of a different estimation of present and future enjoyments as the foundation of the sacrifice of abstinence to be paid for in interest, is a *conditio sine qua non* for the existence of interest. In my opinion, on the other hand, it is not so, because the different estimates placed upon present and future goods, which in any case is necessary for interest, can be, and would be, brought about by the superior productivity of roundabout processes. (See next note.)

[1] For details see 1st ed. of my "Positive Theory of Capital," Smart's translation, p. 260 *sq*. [2] Cf. Marshall, p. 450.

referring to this topic, would furnish grounds for the presumption that he had also adopted the methods of thought peculiar to the use theory.[1] However, in view of the fact that he expresses doubt whether the most outspoken representative of the use theory would wish to teach in all their bearings the principles peculiar to it, I am unable to believe that he himself is inclined to do this, and must rather hold to the presumption that the employment of methods of expression characteristic of the use theory is to be explained by a certain freedom or carelessness of expression which Marshall appears to claim for himself and others on the

[1] pp. 662, 663, 665 *sq.*, and 666, n. In these expressions Marshall repeatedly designates the use or service of capital as the object for which interest is paid, and expressly states that in this connection no essential difference exists between the rent of a durable good (for example, a horse) and the loan of a perishable and replaceable good, such as a sum of money, and adds that the distinction drawn by older writers between renting and lending, though from an analytical point of view interesting, possesses very little practical significance. An entirely similar mingling of expressions (and one to be judged in a similar manner) in which the abstinence theory is represented by terms of expression which seem to point also to the use theory may be found in Sidgwick ("Principles of Political Economy," 2d ed., 1887, pp. 245 *sq.*, 167 *sq.*, and 264).

subject of the theory of interest, notwithstanding the fact that unclearness and ambiguity of expression are responsible for so many mistakes in this field, and notwithstanding the fact that this distinguished scholar is accustomed in other respects to place so great a value upon clearness of conception and fitness of expression of thoughts.

Still another interesting attempt to give a new significance to the old abstinence theory falls within the period under discussion. This was made by an American named Carver,[1] whose discussion shows much discrimination and a remarkable power of combination, but, in my opinion, fails at the critical point on account of a misunderstanding.

His somewhat subtle process of thought, illuminated by a number of geometrical diagrams, may be briefly presented in the following manner.[2] Carver proceeds from the

[1] "The Place of Abstinence in the Theory of Interest" (*Quarterly Journal of Economics*, October, 1893, pp. 40–61).

[2] As a careful reader will soon notice, Carver's process of thought proceeds for a considerable distance parallel with a certain subtle process of reasoning which we have already met in the work of Professor Marshall (see *ante*, p. 44, n. 2). I may,

perfectly correct view, that large quantities of present goods would be saved and devoted to the future even if no interest were received, indeed, even if some expense were involved in their preservation. He also draws the limits of these savings in an entirely correct manner. From his present stock of goods a careful manager will save and devote to the future such a quantity that the marginal utility which the last increment saved, — for example, the last florin, — yields for the future is as great as the utility which the last florin expended for present enjoyment yields. For example, a prudent owner of 100,000 florins of property would certainly not devote the whole or even a very considerable part of this amount to present consumption, even if there were no interest, because in that case he would secure the satisfaction of very unimportant wants, and would reserve no means for satisfying important wants in the future. On the contrary, he

therefore, venture the suggestion that Carver may have received from those expressions of Marshall the first impulse to his theory, which, to be sure, at a certain point takes an entirely different direction.

would stop his present consumption at the point where, with due regard to the streams of goods maturing in the future and available for that period, the marginal utility of the last florin expended equals the future marginal utility of the last florin saved.

Another very important point is also brought out by Carver and correctly illustrated in his diagrams. According to their intellectual tendencies and temperaments, most men are accustomed to underestimate future pleasures and pains and future utilities. A careless or extravagant man, for example, will be inclined at the moment to estimate at a figure perhaps not higher than 10, an enjoyment or a utility to be expected one year hence, which at the moment of its actual appearance will be represented by the figure 15. Now, since our present economic calculations must be determined by our present estimate of the possible satisfactions between which choice may be made, the above-described limits to saving without interest should be modified, since saving will be extended to that point at which the marginal utility of the last florin expended for present satisfactions equals the present estimate of the future marginal utility of the last florin saved. In our example, this limit will be reached if the marginal utility of the last-expended florin, 10, amounts to the future marginal utility of the last-saved florin, that is, 15, which 15 in the present estimation is only equal to the present utility of 10.

In order to throw a still clearer light upon Carver's innovation, I will add that all previous representatives of the abstinence theory have expressed or tacitly connected the sacrifice of abstinence with precisely this last difference. The preference for present enjoyments is, in their eyes, the chief ground why the withholding of enjoyments or the waiting for them is felt to be a sacrifice. The greater that preference, the greater are the obstacles to saving and capital-building, and these can only be overcome in the degree that the sacrifice involved in their removal is adequately remunerated by interest. Thus the height of interest is brought into connection with the strength of the preference for present goods. In conformity with the old abstinence theory, therefore, the difference between the true magnitude of the future utility and its underestimated present amount, represented in our intentionally drastic example by the difference between 15 and 10, appears as the real force which determines interest.

At this point Carver adopts an entirely different line of thought. The existence of the psychological fact which we have just described is recognized and expressly noted by him; but he sees the content of the abstinence which demands remuneration not in it, but in something entirely different. So long as saving has the effect that the present goods transferred to the future yield in the future a utility which in present estimation is more important than that utility which the saved goods could have had in case of their consumption in the present, no sacrifice is connected with it. This part of the accumulation of capital is without cost, and requires, therefore, no interest as a remuneration for sacrifice (p. 49); but real sacrifice begins when the saving should be or must be extended beyond that limit. In our example, for instance, if still more goods should be withdrawn from present enjoyment and transferred to the future, this could only happen on condition that the present satisfaction of those wants which still possess an importance superior to the figure 10 should be discontinued, for example, on condition that the category of wants whose importance lies between the figures 10 and 11 should go unsatisfied. But if the goods withdrawn from the service of the present are added to those provisions for the future which have been accumulated by preceding saving without cost and in the gratification of present wants have already reached the value of 10, this fresh increment can naturally only be applied to the gratification of less important wants, for example, to those the importance of which lies between the figures 10 and 9. The continuance of the process of saving, therefore, leads to the result that a number of goods, which in present use would have yielded a final utility of from 10 to 11, in the future will yield a smaller utility, one estimated according to present calculations between 10 and 9. The difference represents a pure loss caused by the process of saving, a real sacrifice, due to abstinence from present gratification, which cannot and will not be made without an adequate compensation in the form of interest. "The loss in the subjective valuation of this last increment must be compensated for by an increase in objective goods or interest" (p. 53).

If the needs of production could be satisfied with the goods saved without sacrifice, there would be no interest. But if more capital is needed, that is to say, if more capital than that saved without cost can be invested in the gradual exploitation of remunerative opportunities for investment and "still afford profit at the margin," then interest must appear; for then, in order to accumulate the additional savings, somebody must make the previously mentioned sacrifice in subjective value, and this sacrifice demands compensation. For the rate of interest, "the marginal sacrifice of saving" is decisive (p. 53); that is, the magnitude of the last and most costly part of the saving (that part which involves the greatest loss in subjective value) which is needed to satisfy the demands of production.

It is easy to see that the substance of the

abstinence sacrifice which demands compensation in interest is explained by Carver in a manner entirely different from that of the other abstinence theorists. The latter put the emphasis upon the fact that man, as he is constituted, dislikes waiting for gratifications. Carver, on the other hand, does not find the sacrifice in a postponement of gratification, but in the further circumstance, conditionally connected therewith, that on account of the disposition to save, the relation between wants and the means for their satisfaction is so disturbed that the same quantity of goods has less final utility and value in the future than in the present. Carver sees the essence of the sacrifice not in the fact that the gratification comes later, but that it is *smaller* than the present one, its rival. The difference in the essence of the sacrifice may easily be represented by the figures of our example. Whereas, in the first case, the difference between the real value of a future gratification and the present estimation of it would be registered in our example by the figures 15 and 10, the value of Carver's sacrifice of abstinence is represented by the difference between 11 and 9, a result wholly different and due to causes other than those which explain the difference between the last use realized in the present and the present value of the last use realized in the future.

But it is further easy to see that Carver has mistaken an effect of interest for its cause. All the facts that he presents are perfectly correct, even the one regarding the decrease of final utility[1] in case a future period should be better endowed with funds than the present; but he confounds cause and effect. Not because and in the same measure as the future is better endowed does interest appear or the rate increase, but just the reverse. Interest must be an actual fact, in order that there may be an economic cause for a better endowment of the future; and the higher interest is, the more this endowment may be increased. If, and because, the rate of interest is 5 per cent, the endowment of the future may reasonably be increased to such an extent that 105 pieces of goods in the following year will yield

[1] I have myself drawn attention to this phenomenon (see my "Positive Theory," 1st ed., p. 446).

the same utility as 100 at present; if, and because, interest is at the rate of 20 per cent, the endowment of the future may be increased until 120 pieces in the following year yield the same utility as 100 at present (always referring to the present estimation), and so on.

On the other hand, that other psychological fact in which the abstinence theorists see the essence of the sacrifice of abstinence, has a share in the origin of interest. The disposition of people so much to prefer immediate enjoyment to future gratification that they place a future pleasure of the value of 15 on a par with a present one of the value of 10, is indeed the real cause why the goods produced for the future should obtain and maintain a value in excess of their cost. With that disposition, producers cannot be inclined to incur a greater expense than 10 for the acquisition of a product that will in time have a value of 15, but which in their present estimation is worth only 10. The completion of the process of production will yield, after the expiration of a year, a product of the actual value of 15, against which there are costs of production of the value of 10 only. Hence, a surplus, or an interest of 5, results. Indeed, this surplus will result, even if Carver's sacrifice of abstinence is not taken into account at all, provided that only such a quantity of goods is devoted to the future as, according to the present estimate, will make a single unit both in the present and the future yield a marginal utility of 10.

And even the removal of that surplus of value by competition would under these circumstances be effectually opposed by the same motive that produced it, without the necessity of the appearance or of the operation of Carver's sacrifice of abstinence. If, for example, by a temporary increase of production the objective value of the product should be diminished from 15 to 14, this 14, so long as the coefficient of undervaluation remains the same, would be thought equal to a smaller amount than 10, namely to about 9.3. If, as supposed, goods devoted to present consumption fall to a final utility of 10, their employment for the acquisition of a pleasure valued at 9.3 would evidently appear uneconomical. The category of present wants, the importance of which is under 10 but above 9.3, would be preferred to the less remunerative expenditure for the future; and, in consequence, smaller means would be reserved for future use, the production of future good diminished, and their value finally enhanced until the former relation, indicated by an objective value of 15, equal in present estimation to present final utility of 10, be reëstablished, and with it a surplus in value of 5. If interest has once been called into existence by these forces, it will follow as a normal consequence that people will endow the future somewhat more richly than they would have done if there had been no interest, and this will give rise to the phenomenon noticed by Carver of the falling of the present estimate of the future marginal utility of a unit of goods below its present utility, which, of course, is not the same thing as the falling of its real marginal utility. But all this is entirely a consequence of interest. It may be that a secondary reaction on the rate of interest will emanate from it; but it is to be observed that this reaction will be exerted in the direction of a reduction of interest, and the rôle of intermediary cause will doubtless fall to the increased intensity of the motive to saving, but by no means to Carver's sacrifice of abstinence, which would manifest itself in exactly the opposite direction, namely, in increased saving, which richly endows the future, and therefore presses down the marginal utility of the savings.

This brings me to the point at which, perhaps, Carver's misconception can be most clearly illustrated. Without any question, interest arises from the scarcity of capital, which means the same thing as the scarcity of means of gratification devoted to the future. Carver, on the contrary, comes to the conclusion that it is the result of the abundance of these gratifications, the consequence of a sort of plethora of saving. The true place which the facts, quite correctly observed by Carver, occupy in the chain of causes is well indicated by the following parallel: Just as a rise in the value of money, caused by a money stringency, is accustomed to bring forth a secondary stream, which tends to weaken the intensity of the stringency, this secondary stream being due to the well-known fact that the high purchasing power of money attracts to the mint quantities of precious metals which had till then been used as jewellery, plate, and so on, and thereby increases the supply of money,— so interest, caused by scarcity of capital, by the very fact of its existence produces a secondary movement which tends to modify its own magnitude by causing an extension of saving beyond the point at which it would otherwise have stopped. Now, one is no more correct in regarding the over-saving caused by the existence of interest and the accompanying fact of diminished final utility as the principal power which produces interest and fixes its rate than he would be in considering the increased output of gold and silver coins as the real cause of the rise in the value of gold.

So far, therefore, as the subject of "abstinence" comes under consideration in the explanation of interest, I think I must give the older interpretation of the abstinence theory, at least relatively, the preference over Carver's new one. The former at least had in view the correct fundamental phenomenon which really coöperates as a primary force in the causation of interest, though it is mistaken in interpreting and representing the manner of that coöperation. Carver, on the contrary, has been misled by an ingenious but erroneous combination of ideas, and has taken the wrong track, in that he pursues a phenomenon which is merely an accompaniment and a result of interest instead of its real cause.[1]

[1] It is interesting to observe that Carver, like Macfarlane, regards my own interest theory as in substance an abstinence theory (with elements of the theory of productivity added), agrees with it in substance, and believes that he has presented it in a more intelligible, and in some respects a more correct, way. "With certain corrections, which will be noticed later," he says, speaking of my theory, "his theory may be regarded as correct; but it is to be hoped that the interest problem can be explained upon principles more easily understood by the average reader" (p. 44). His own and Macfarlane's example, in addition to the eminently sagacious and yet unsatisfactory explanations of prominent scientists like Jevons and Marshall, furnishes an exceedingly instructive illustration of the manifold ramifications of which the conception of the apparently simple relation of present and future is capable. It also shows that it is no superfluous pedantry on my part if in criticism and in positive theory I do not rest satisfied with mere references to the "prospectiveness" and "productiveness" of capital, but insist that these notions shall receive a perfectly definite meaning, one by which alone they are capable of fitting into a really decisive and essentially and logically correct explanation of our phenomenon.

CHAPTER V

LABOUR THEORIES

In my "Capital and Interest" (Part I) I have described three different types of the labour theory. The first of these, which in former times was represented by James Mill and McCulloch, so far as I know has found no representative in recent times, and may, therefore, be considered as dead and buried.[1]

The second type, the French form of the labour theory, which regards interest as the compensation for the moral effort of saving, so far as I can perceive, has received no new reënforcements, though it holds its own within the narrow circle of its former adherents.

As for the third form of this theory, that which declares interest to be a kind of official

[1] Though Giddings's theory, which we have briefly considered in another place (see above, p. 11), bears a certain resemblance to this type, yet his standpoint is theoretically so different and so much more advanced that I preferred to range his theory in another and more modern group.

income paid to the class of capitalists as a salary for the social function of accumulating and employing capital, it may be observed as a remarkable literary fact of the most recent times, that Adolf Wagner, whom I have conditionally ranged in this group, has now emphatically declared that he does not accept the labour theory as a sufficient theoretical explanation of the phenomenon of interest, and that those expressions of his which resemble the process of thought peculiar to this theory relate only to the socio-political view of interest, that is, to the question of its justification. Regarding the peculiarly theoretical problem of interest Wagner declares himself in agreement with the essential points of my explanation.[1] Stolzmann,[2] on the other hand, has accepted and elaborately defended this type of the labour theory. Since his work exhibits many original features, and certainly represents the most carefully and closely thought-out form of this theory, a somewhat

[1] "Grundlegung," 3d ed., Pt. II, p. 289 *sq.*

[2] "Die sociale Kategorie in der Volkswirtschaftslehre," Berlin, 1896.

more thorough exposition and consideration of it is in place here.

Stolzmann makes the theory of value his starting-point. He represents a peculiar modification of the labour-cost theory. According to him the exchange value of goods is determined by their labour-cost, but not, as Ricardo and the Socialists teach, by the quantity of labour employed in the production of goods, nor, as other theorists have been teaching, by the amount of displeasure and trouble connected with that labour; but he holds that labour is the decisive cause of value, because and to the extent that it requires remuneration, and that, therefore, it is not so much labour itself, as its wages, that determine value (p. 335). But wages themselves, and this is the second fundamental premise of Stolzmann's system, are determined by the relative power of social groups (Sociale Machtverhältnisse). The labourer must live. In every period of his existence he needs a certain quantity of provisions (this term being used in its widest sense), and this quantity Stolzmann calls the "unit of provisions" (Nahrungsmitteleinheit).

To this notion he attributes extraordinary importance. It appears to him to be an indispensable, intermediary link in the formation and determination of the value of goods. Starting from the widely spread notion that individual wants are incommensurable,[1] he thinks that the value of goods cannot be derived from or measured by them; that, on the contrary, in this, as in every other scientific question, man with all his needs must be considered as a single whole, as the unit which influences value at first hand (p. 264). The process by which value is determined, therefore, is about as follows: First of all, the magnitude of "the unit of provisions" which the working-man is able to acquire for himself is determined by social forces. This unit is not a fixed quantity established by physiology or by any law of nature, but the result of a social struggle, in which not purely economic causes, but the relative power of the contending forces decides what quantity of provisions

[1] I have criticised this opinion in another place (Conrad's *Jahrbücher*, N.F., Vol. XIII, p. 46 *sq.*). Here I wish to avoid criticism, and will therefore not examine the point further at this time.

the labourer obtains, what standard of life he can maintain. From the magnitude of the unit of provisions the value of goods is derived by the simple rule that a product is always worth as many units of provisions as there were units of time (for example, days of labour) or aliquot parts of units of time required for its production.

Stolzmann develops this "law of labour-cost," first of all, for a hypothetical, primitive type of society. He assumes a social group of ten persons who procure their ten units of provisions upon a common plan by division of labour. They are supposed to be equal in diligence and ability, and each of them applies himself to the production of one of the ten species of goods of which every unit is composed, and, during one and the same period, manufactures ten pieces from the beginning to the end. Under these circumstances, Stolzmann continues, no other division of the produce could take place than that based on the principle that each should receive, for the unit of labour which he had contributed to production, just one unit of provisions, composed of one piece of each of the ten kinds; and the several pieces of every kind, if they should be exchanged at all, would be exchanged on an equal basis, since each of them is produced by the same number of labour units and represents the same number of units of provisions. Why? Because, according to our assumption, all the ten partners are equipotent; no one of them is subjected to any sort of compulsion or coercion, but each one, by threatening to "run away," is in a condition effectually to oppose any attempt on the part of his colleagues to restrict him to a smaller unit of provisions or to reward him according to a worse standard for the goods produced.[1]

With certain modifications Stolzmann then transfers this law of labour-cost, made plausible for a primitive community, to developed society. Here distribution is by far more complicated, partly because the units of provisions are not nowadays constituted by simply bringing together their component parts, but by complicated processes of exchange, and partly because labourers are not the only participants in the

[1] pp. 31–36; see also p. 304.

distribution of the produce, but must compete also with capitalists and landowners. But the essence of the process of distribution remains the same. Stolzmann repeatedly rejects, with the greatest possible emphasis, the idea that each of the agents of production is remunerated according to its contribution to the whole produce, and that economic causes or the technique of production are decisive in the determination of the shares in distribution. Indeed, his entire work, as its very title, "The Social Category," shows, is an attempt to prove that the actual distribution of goods at the present time is determined, not by purely economic, but by "social forces." To quote some characteristic sayings: "Power alone, the laws governing distribution, determine the magnitude of the shares in distribution" (p. 41). "The technical contribution of the factor, nature, differs very materially from its social contribution and share of income" (p. 341 *sq.*). "Not what any agent of production contributes towards the technique of production, but the dividend which can and must be given to its proprietor for its surrender, is decisive for the amount of his share in the distribution" (p. 338). The value of the whole is distributed among the proprietors of the three factors of production, not in proportion to the share which each has had in the production, but "according to principles essentially different, *i.e.* according to the relative amounts of social power each exerts" (p. 61), and in the following manner: The working-man desires and needs his "worker's unit of provisions." How large this is does not depend, as other theorists believe, on the productive effect of labour, but essentially on "the existing social class relations." "The traditional standard of life of the working classes, their power, their covetousness, and the esteem they enjoy as fellow-men, according to the opinions regarding human dignity and the precepts of ethics and religion held at the time," determine the rate of wages they can obtain (p. 334). But the capitalist also desires to live. He desires and needs his "capitalist's unit of provisions," the amount of which, like that of the worker's unit, is determined by social forces, such as the level of culture, the extent of their fashionable wants, their previous education, the extent to which they coöperate through unions, trusts, and syndicates, the intervention of the State, and the like (p. 371 *sq.*). Particularly decisive for the rate of profit is the standard of life of the "last," that is, the least important capitalist, as determined by such social conditions; in other words, to capital must be given such a per cent of profit as will yield the capitalist's unit of provisions even to the least important capitalist who can just stand the competition but is still indispensable to the production of the supplies needed by society.

Thus are determined the elements of exchange value in modern society. The exchange value of goods fixes itself at that level which is required to remunerate the labour employed in their production at the rate of wages enforced by the labourers, and the coöperating capital at the rate of profit necessary for supplying the capitalist's unit of provisions. The landowner, on the contrary, appears merely as a "residual claimant"; he receives as the rent of land "the portion which remains after deducting the two first fixed quotas from the total receipts."

But how can this theory of value claim to be a "labour-cost theory," when it recognizes as an independent element in the formation of value, besides labour and the wages of labour, also the service of the capital which must be remunerated? This difficulty is surmounted by declaring the work of capitalists remunerated by interest to be a kind of labour. At the very close of his systematic presentation, Stolzmann makes this declaration when he explains profits as the "socially necessary remuneration for the socially indispensable function of forming and employing capital." This, he says, is no new idea, but one that agrees in its essence with that conception which we have designated as the German type of the labour-cost theory of interest. Stolzmann quotes with approval an utterance of Adolf Wagner, according to which the "labour" constituting the cost of production comprises also the necessary services of private capitalists and employers, and emphatically declares that upon this idea he wishes to base, not merely, as in Wagner's case, the social and political justification of interest, but also its theoretical explanation (p. 421 *sq.*). Stolzmann did not keep in sight during the whole course of his work the necessary consequences of this theory. There are passages in which he seems to hold that the labour-cost which determines value, consists of the "worker's unit of provisions" in a narrow sense.[1] But Stolzmann's real view does not seem to me to be represented by such casual utterances as are inconsistent with his principles, but rather by such statements as promote the capitalist's function to the dignity of a species of labour in need of remuneration.

In my opinion Stolzmann's theory in all its

[1] *E.g.* p. 330, where he says, Capital is identical in value with the labour-cost employed in it, and labour-cost is identical with the workers' units of provisions paid as wages to the labourers. Similarly, pp. 372 and 378, where he works it out numerically. I observe also that these utterances are not based upon the assumption of a primitive, non-capitalistic state of society, but that the existence of capital in a developed community is assumed. In my review of Stolzmann's book, in the *Zeitschrift für Volkswirtschaft, Socialpolitik und Verwaltung*, Vol. VII, p. 424, it was passages like these which caused me to reproach Stolzmann with ignoring the influence of unequal expenditures of time on the formation of value. Upon renewed reflection, however, I think that these utterances were mere oversights, and that Stolzmann's real opinion is the one expounded in the text.

parts is open to numerous objections. What I have said in the proper place against labour theories in general, naturally applies to Stolzmann's theory as well as the others, and I will not repeat it here. I will content myself with pointing out the most striking weaknesses of the special form which he has given to the theory.

First of all, the very foundation of the whole system, the labour-cost theory of value, is without any solid basis. He endeavours to make plausible his contention that labour-cost is the only possible foundation of value by an example taken from primitive society. In this he commits a mistake, peculiarly interesting on account of its relation to a previous discussion of his. He had justly blamed Ricardo for deducing his well-known law of value from an arbitrarily constructed primitive type of society, without noticing the fact that the correspondence of value with the quantity of labour employed was only the result of the accidental circumstances of his arbitrarily constructed type of primitive society. But in the same breath Stolzmann commits precisely the same error by the threefold supposition that all the members of a primitive society are equally industrious and skilful, and apply their labour during productive periods of the same length.[1] He, too, has eliminated from his example any circumstance that might cause the value of the product to deviate from parallelism, not only with Ricardo's labour-quantities, but also with his own labour-costs, or force it to conform to a standard other than this. And for the very same reason Stolzmann's key to distribution is only "a chance peculiarity of this special hypothesis," and no universally valid, theoretical fact. Had Stolzmann introduced into his hypothesis unequally skilful or unequally industrious partners, he would certainly have quickly convinced himself that, even in the absence of relations tend-

[1] This third supposition is not made expressly, but it is clearly implied in the assumption, on the one hand, that every partner produces one commodity "from beginning to end," and thus measures off the entire production period, and, on the other hand, that "for every period of consumption" the same number of pieces of each kind is "available for consumption," so that evidently the periods of production and the periods of consumption must be equal to each other. A passage confirming this view may be found on page 32.

ing to coerce the labourer, full and equal units of provisions are not always to be realized, and that a very important part[1] of what he is inclined to treat under the head of "force" is derived from no other source than the economic efficiency of the respective factors of production. It is very easy to see why the threat of an idle or unskilful worker to "run away" will exercise a much less efficient power in securing for him a large unit of provisions than the same threat of a skilful and industrious worker!

The situation is precisely the same regarding the different lengths of the periods of time which intervene between the beginning of labour and the acquisition of its fruits, and during which every one must wait. In Stolzmann's primitive society no regard for these intervals of time can interfere with the labour-costs key which he has discovered,

[1] A very important part, but not the whole. Upon the problems which exist along this line, and which still persist in spite of the solution attempted by Stolzmann in his one-sided exaggeration, I have expressed myself in my above-mentioned review of his book, *Zeitschrift für Volkswirthschaft, Socialpolitik und Verwaltung*, Vol. VII, p. 425 *sq*.

since they are assumed to be the same for all labourers and for all sorts of production, thus mutually offsetting each other. But Stolzmann cannot and evidently does not claim that this equality of intervals of time is actually to be met with in real life; certainly he will not claim that it is so universally met with that it may be regarded as a typical, normal case, from which a universally valid law may be derived. Just as little can he assume without proof that the diversity of these intervals is without influence on the formation of value. But he actually does make this assumption.

He touches upon this question in that portion of his book (p. 303) in which he states that the work done in advance is substantially equal to that done afterward, and that the difference between these kinds of labour is "nothing but" a difference in time, which in his primitive community exerts "no appreciable influence upon value and distribution." As the same quantity of labour is at stake in both cases, that performed in advance and that performed afterward must be regarded as equal for purposes of distribution. According to his notion, time can play a part in the formation of value and in distribution in the form of labour-time only, and hence "the value to be allotted to the several labourers as multiples or aliquot parts of units of provisions must be proportioned to the length of time which is put in by the several labourers," without any reference to the question whether the labour was performed in advance or afterward. I think all this is simply a presumption contrary to facts, which reminds us of Marx's[1] unproved denial of the influence of the time spent in waiting, and which indicates a *petitio principii* invoked by both authors in favour of the principle of value which each holds.[2]

[1] See my "Geschichte und Kritik der Capitalzins-Theorien," 2d ed., p. 554 *sq*.

[2] In a strange way Stolzmann tries to turn my argument against me, and reproaches me with a *petitio principii*, notwithstanding my rather explicit demonstration that not only the time of labour but also the time of waiting is a circumstance by no means irrelevant in the explanation of remuneration and valuation. I do not intend here to make a rejoinder, for which, perhaps, a more suitable place may be found in the second volume of this work. I will only remark that all the attempts of Stolzmann to explain away the necessity of "waiting" by a skilful interlapping of stages of production and needs ("Sociale Kategorie,"

The unnatural character of Stolzmann's conception, resulting from the fact that he stamps a manifest proprietor's revenue as a species of wages of labour, I need not demonstrate again after all that I have said on this point in my treatment of labour theories in general.

Stolzmann seems to me to be wholly in error in his attempt to attribute to the capitalist's unit of provisions the importance of a determining cause in the processes of distribution and the formation of capital. If there is anything that is not the *cause* of the existence or of the height of interest, but its *effect*, that is surely the standard of life of capitalists. There is no minimum of property with regard to which one could say that any

p. 304 *sq.*, especially 307, 308, 313), even under the hypothesis of longer periods of production, seem to me utterly fallacious and futile. Even the most skilful manipulation cannot make a cover longer than it is, and if Stolzmann honestly believes that it is legitimate to assume that even then "a sufficient quantity of present goods will always be ready for immediate consumption" (p. 313), so that society will be relieved of the burden of waiting, this "sufficient quantity of present goods" in his process of thought plays the rôle of a *deus ex machina*. Their "always being ready" would certainly solve all difficulties, but neither their "readiness" nor their certain "sufficiency" is explained.

technical need of production or any other socio-economic necessity requires that it must support its owner with a fixed rate of income. A nation needs capital, and so long as the formation of capital is predominantly effected by private economy it also needs capitalists; but it is by no means in need of these to such an extent that it must maintain any person or any class of persons by means of a fixed rate of income on capital. Whoever possesses too little capital of his own to enable him to live on the revenue derived from it in the manner which he considers required by his rank is not on this account obliged to withdraw from his "class" (if by "class" be not meant the group of perfectly idle capitalists, a group certainly not absolutely necessary to the economy of any nation) or to be deprived of his economic existence, but he can very well earn what is lacking by employing or augmenting his personal activity. In fact this is done by the proprietor of a small capital who seeks for employment as an official or a physician or a menial servant, and the same thing is done by the employer who does not confine himself to the general direction of his enterprises, but works in it with his own hands, and by performing the functions of a director or foreman or a simple workman earns in his own enterprise, as it were, also a salary or a wage.

Stolzmann himself had observed a number of difficulties connected with his doctrine regarding the influence of the unit of provisions of the last capitalist, namely, that capitalists, and especially the least important of them, such as labourers, artisans, or officials, are also people who need not live on the revenue of their capital; that the capitalist is not identical with the employer; that the idle capitalist is not a social necessity; that if the entrepreneur rather than the money-lender be regarded as the decisive personality, he is not accustomed to work with his own capital alone, so that in this case the capital of the last employer would not coincide with the amount of capital employed in the last enterprise, and so on. Stolzmann accompanies the review of these difficulties with a very frank recognition of their magnitude. He is forced to admit that when one faces the complete reality, "difficulties quite insuperable" stand in the way of his conception, and that especially the relation, lying at the basis of his conception, between the material and the personal factor, that is, between capital as the factor of production, and the personal proprietor of the same, the capitalist, "seems either not to exist or to be very accidental and loose" (p. 380). In discussing details he finds one of these difficulties "very serious," at first sight even "almost overwhelming"; another is characterized as "still much worse"; again another causes him "almost to doubt" the exactness of his theory; while still another makes it appear "absurd," and so on. Nevertheless he thinks himself able to steer his course among all the cliffs which start up in his way by means of a system of artificial explanations and bold deductions, with which, I at least believe, only one who possesses as great a predilection for the standpoint defended by Stolzmann as the author himself will be inclined to be satisfied. I, therefore, think a detailed criticism unnecessary, and content myself with the two following remarks: —

First, Stolzmann has not kept in view a certain difficulty which would probably have demonstrated the untenableness of his standpoint more strikingly than anything else could have done. This difficulty lies in the circumstance that the magnitude of the entrepreneur's capital varies greatly, not only between enterprises of various sizes within the same branch of business, but also for technical reasons between one branch of production and another, *e.g.* between a gun foundery and the trade of a craftsman or a pedler, and that the magnitude of the capital of the smallest entrepreneur[1] capable of competition, which according to Stolzmann is decisive for the capitalist's unit of provisions, is extraordinarily small. A tailor in some little place may carry on quite a prosperous enter-

[1] The notion of the "last employer" is somewhat ambiguous in itself and also in Stolzmann's book. It may refer to the capitalist who by severe economy is just able to endure competition or to the smallest capitalist, *i.e.* the one working prosperously with the smallest capital. The whole trend of Stolzmann's teaching, as well as numerous expressions pointing in this direction (*e.g.* pp. 381, 383, 390 *sq.*, 396 *sq.*), leave no doubt in my mind that the second interpretation is the one Stolzmann had in mind. To be sure, in one instance, in a parenthetical phrase he expressly explains "the smallest" as the "least favoured" undertaking (p. 396).

prise on the basis of a capital of 100 florins, either of his own or partly or altogether borrowed, but will any one seriously claim that the level of profits in a nation or the rate of interest, let us say the question of its being fixed at 4 or 4½ per cent, will be determined by the fact that this man and such as he need for a living such as is usual in their class 4½ instead of 4 florins per annum! In order to forestall any objection, let me add one other remark. A doubt might arise as to whether, according to Stolzmann's theory, the capitalist employer's unit of provisions must be exclusively supplied from profits on capital, or whether in the calculation the whole income of the employer is taken into account. Practically this difference, especially important in the case of the smaller and least important employers, would show itself in the taking or not taking into account of those parts of revenue which are earned by personal labour such as could be performed by paid employers or helpers.

Stolzmann does not expressly decide this question in his final and formal definition of the "last capitalist." He defines this personage (p. 396) as the "proprietor of a stock of capital by means of which and the credit based on it he is able to establish and prosperously to carry on the last still competing enterprise in such a way that by means of the value of its produce he may be able to defray the expense not only of the wear and tear of capital and of the wages of labour, but also of the minimum standard of life usual with employers of the time, and of the interest on the capital borrowed." With this definition one must still ask whether Stolzmann means by the "wages of labour" only those paid to other men or also those earned by the employer himself. In my opinion, the whole tendency of Stolzmann's theory here demands the narrower interpretation of the term "wages of labour," so that wages earned by the employer himself are to be considered not as a part of the expense to be deducted beforehand, but as a part of the capitalist's unit of provisions remaining after the deduction of expenses. But Stolzmann's theory comes to grief whichever signification he adopts. If he does not choose to reckon, in the socially necessary unit of provisions, the personal earnings of the entrepreneur, it means that in our neither fanciful nor impossible example of the tailor with 100 florins of capital and 4 or even 10 or 20 florins of profits, he maintains that the standard of life usual to the class of poor, independent craftsmen can be nowadays maintained with 4, 10, or 20 florins yearly; or, in manifest opposition to facts, that enterprises of such insignificance as not to afford a bare competence without the master's manual labour cannot exist; in other words, that the economy of nature requires that even the class of the smallest entrepreneurs shall be made up of capitalist employers who do not themselves labour. But if Stolzmann chooses to count these earnings as a part of the unit of provisions, not as wages of labour but as profits of capital, he arrives necessarily at the absurd conclusion that our little tailor, who certainly earns by his business every year more than some hundred florins, receives from his capital of 100 florins a profit of some hundreds per cent, and that this monstrous rate of profit is to be regarded as the general one of that time and nation as determined by the last capitalist's earnings. Or, finally, he may choose to count the personal earnings of the last capitalist as a part of his unit of provisions, and at the same time recognize them as wages. I may observe, by the way, that this is most likely Stolzmann's meaning, although on one occasion and in a passage which purports to be a definition, he expresses himself in a manner incompatible with this interpretation.[1] But if this be Stolzmann's opinion, he has evidently completely failed in his explanation and demonstration. He wished to show that the rate of profits is determined by the capitalist's unit of provisions. But if, besides the profit of capital, some

[1] On page 396 may be found the following passage emphasized by italics: "The rate of profit which the last entrepreneur receives is the percentage which expresses the numerical proportion of his own capital to the socially necessary entrepreneur's unit of provisions." Here the rate of profit is deduced from the proportion of the whole entrepreneur's unit to his own capital, and thereby this entire unit is regarded as profits. On the contrary, his remark that interest sometimes constitutes a determinate fraction of profits (397), and that "great and small capitalists receive the same percentage of profit" (380), leads to the conclusion that he was not willing to regard the whole income of an employer as profits on capital, but as a heterogeneous aggregate including some earnings of labour. However, on this, as well as many other decisive points, Stolzmann's theory is obscure.

other thing, such as the earnings of labour, is or can be included in the unit of provisions, even if this unit were itself real, and were able to determine anything whatever, at best it could only determine how much the smallest capitalist-employer must receive from two different sources together; but as these two sources can be combined in all possible proportions, the part which profits have in that mixture, — the real object of the whole inquiry, — remains completely undetermined. Moreover, Stolzmann has not even tried to demonstrate, — what indeed cannot be demonstrated at all, — that between these two sources there must be some socially necessary proportion, and that the share of the capitalist must accordingly be a quantity determined by a social necessity and itself ruling the whole capital market. Such an attempt at demonstration, not to speak of other difficulties, would be refuted by the simple case of the little tailor which shows that the part which capital occupies in the total income of the smallest entrepreneur is relatively trifling, a veritable *quantité négligeable;* and one could not avoid the absurdity that to gradations within this evidently insignificant *quantité négligeable* must be ascribed the all-decisive rôle in the world of capital.

In conclusion I must not omit to mention that Stolzmann's treatment in individual cases often attracts me by its freshness and originality, as well as by the evident energy of his spirit of investigation; but as for its positive results, I regard them as so unsatisfactory that I do not expect them to play an influential part in the future history of theories of interest.

CHAPTER VI

THE PRODUCTIVITY THEORIES

THE number of those theorists who in recent times have professed in a pure or an eclectic form an indirect productivity theory is far from being insignificant. Without any pretension to completeness, I may mention from the literature of the Romance nations Maurice Block[1] and Maffeo Pantaleoni,[2] from the Anglo-American literature Francis Walker,[3] and from the German once more Dietzel, who with a peculiarly eclectic method would explain a portion of the phenomena of interest by the

[1] "Progrès de la science économique depuis Ad. Smith" (Paris, 1890), II, pp. 319 *sq.*, 328, 335 *sq.*

[2] "Principii di Economia pura," Florence, 1889 (2d ed. unchanged, 1894), p. 301. Pantaleoni's theory, but briefly indicated, seems to move wholly in the course of Wieser's views, which will be more amply criticised further on.

[3] *Quarterly Journal of Economics*, July, 1892. See also my reply, *ibid.*, April, 1895.

exploitation theory and the rest by the theory of productivity,[1] then Philippovich,[2] Diehl,[3] Julius Wolf,[4] and Wieser.[5]

The greater number of these authors confine themselves within the bounds of this type of theory, or do not step out of them far enough to admit of a reproduction and criticism of their views in detail without tedious repetitions of well-known ideas.[6] There is only

[1] See Chapter VIII of this book.

[2] "Grundriss der politischen Ökonomie," 2d ed., § 121.

[3] P. J. Proudhon, "Seine Lehre und sein Leben," II. Abth., Jena, 1890, pp. 216–225.

[4] "Socialismus und capitalistische Gesellschaftsordnung," Stuttgart, 1892.

[5] "Der natürliche Wert," Vienna, 1889.

[6] This is also true of the explanations of Wolf, which, though very explicit, are to my mind very obscure. He maintains "the value-productivity of capital," but in proof contents himself with reflections which I cannot regard as real explanations or solid arguments, but only as paraphrases of the problem. He describes the "value-productivity of capital," the existence of which he is attempting to prove, as "the capacity of capital to furnish a revenue exceeding (*a*) its own costs, and (*b*) the costs of those factors of production which are technically able eventually to replace the capital consumed"; and he wishes to support his affirmation by the well-known fact that a balance of the kind mentioned shows itself whenever by the intervention of capital the advantages of the division of labour, of production on a large scale, of machinery, and of natural forces, the employment of which demands an investment of some kind, are obtained.

one of these theories which seems to me to justify a special examination, and that is Wieser's.

Wieser has put science under lasting obli-

"Capital," says Wolf, "is doubtless an objective intermediary of productivity" (p. 461 *sq.*).

That capital acts as an "intermediary" in the production of surplus-value cannot be doubted. This is indeed the reason why this surplus-value has in general been theoretically and practically considered as the income from capital or the interest on capital, and not as wages of labour or entrepreneur's profits. But precisely this is the substance of the interest problem, the fact to be explained by any theory of interest, and by no means a proof or an evidence of the correctness of any specific theory, for example, of that one which attributes value-productivity to capital. In the polemical parts of his argument, Wolf himself feels the necessity of amplifying the above explanation. He thinks, for example, that the consumer will necessarily have to value the quantity of the product, increased perhaps fourfold by the employment of capital, higher than the capital consumed, in order to offer "the producer any inducement for employing his capital at all"; and that the consumer will be ready to put this increased valuation upon the product "because by so doing he can share in the advantages of the operations of capital, without which he would be obliged to pay fourfold as much for the fourfold increased quantity of product, whereas now he pays only double or treble as much. Therefore, he who decides the value of goods, the consumer, by force of reason, in order to derive advantage from the employment of capital, is obliged to leave more to the capitalist than the mere equivalent of his expenses, and thus to afford him an interest upon his capital." In this way the productivity of goods passes over into a productivity of value (p. 466). But in all other cases, efficient competition being granted, reason is accustomed so to govern the

gations to him for his thorough investigation[1] into the general relations between the value of cost goods and that of their products, as well as by his unsurpassably clear explanation of the fact that the problem of the imputation of value to the agents which coöperate in the production of a good is essentially different from that of the determination of the physical contribution of each to the common product; and that this problem is not practically or theoretically insolvable.[2] Wieser seems to me to have been somewhat less fortunate in the positive formulation of his attempt at the solution of this problem, and especially in his application of the theory of imputation to the explanation of interest. In my opinion this is chiefly due to the fact that he has not

actions of both parties on the market that the price of goods is brought to a level with the costs of their production. The reduction of cost is transformed into a decline of prices. Why should not this be the case here, or at least up to a certain point? This puzzle needs a clearer explanation than the allusion to Adam Smith's old-fashioned truism that capitalists need interest, in order to have a motive for employing capital!

[1] "Ueber den Ursprung und die Hauptgesetze des wirtschaftlichen Wertes," Vienna, 1884, p. 139 *sq.*; "Der natürliche Wert," Vienna, 1889, pp. 67 *sq.*, 164 *sq.*

[2] "Der natürliche Wert," § 20.

remained completely true to his own theoretical assumptions, but has passed over to a train of reasoning which in its essence is unfit to solve the problem, and clashes with the other premises of his theory.

In his model exposition of the imputation problem, Wieser starts from the assumption that the economic part which each of the several coöperating factors has in the common product (Wieser names this the "productive contribution") can be calculated and separated, and that the value of the productive goods is derived from the magnitude of the shares assigned them in such a manner that the whole value of the product[1] (determined according to the law of marginal utility) is distributed among all the productive goods coöperating in its production, the part of each factor in the whole value depending upon the size of its "productive contribution," and the sum of all "productive contributions" exactly exhausting the value of the product.[2]

The manner in which, according to Wieser's

[1] "Der natürliche Wert," p. 96 *sq.*

[2] *Ibid.*, p. 85 *sq.*, especially pp. 87, 90, 91, 92.

opinion, the amount of the productive contribution of each factor is to be found, need not be explained here. Important as this question may be for other problems, for the solution which Wieser tries to give to the interest problem, it is irrelevant. For our present purpose it is sufficient to remember that, according to Wieser, products as a rule result from the coöperation of land, capital, and labour, and that a certain part of the total is to be assigned to each of these factors and thus also to the factor capital as its productive contribution. The fact that pure interest results from the imputation of a share to capital depends, according to Wieser's opinion, — an opinion which in this particular is surely justified, — not upon the question whether the productive contribution of capital is higher or lower as compared to those of land and labour, but upon forces which operate exclusively within the province of capital.

"Every capital," he says, "yields at first and immediately only a gross return, that is, a product obtained by a diminution of its substance."[1]

[1] "Der natürliche Wert," p. 123.

The conditions under which this gross return can become the source of a net income, Wieser formulates in the statement that in the gross product all the consumed parts of capital must be reproduced and a surplus be present in addition. And with reference to this surplus and the "productivity of the capital" directed toward its production, one must distinguish between a *physical* surplus and the *physical* productivity of capital on the one hand and a surplus of *value* and a *value-productivity* of capital on the other. Whoever wishes to solve the problem of interest must, in the last analysis, prove the existence of a *value-productivity* in capital, and explain it. But in this proof the demonstration of the physical productivity of capital[1] forms a necessary intermediary link. Accordingly, Wieser gives his explanation in

[1] "The problem of the theory finally is to prove 'the value-productivity of capital'; but for this purpose, first of all, the physical productivity of capital must be proved, the latter being the stepping-stone to the former. Value-productivity presupposes the determination of the value of the capital, but you can only reach the determination of the value of capital after having answered the question how to calculate the physical share of capital in the product, because the value of capital rests on the physical share attributed to it in the product."

two stages. In the first his aim is to prove and explain the "physical productivity of capital" or the fact that "the *quantity* of goods contained in the gross return of capital is greater than the *quantity* of productive goods consumed in the process of production." In the second stage it remains to be explained why "the *value* of the gross return is greater than that of the consumed capital." The first part of his process of reasoning is as follows:—

"Unquestionably the whole return of the three factors of production, land, labour, and capital, taken together, is large enough to replace the consumed capital and to give a net product. This is an economic fact which is as notorious and as little in need of proof as the fact, for example, that there are goods and that there is production. Sometimes, it is true, an enterprise of production proves to be a failure and does not meet its expenses; there are even undertakings which yield no available product at all; but these are exceptions. The rule is that net returns are obtained, yes, net returns of the greatest extent, so that more than a thousand millions of men are maintained, and additions to capital continually made. But one question, therefore, can be asked, namely, whether a part of these unquestioned net returns is also to be ascribed to capital; but the answer to this question cannot be doubtful. Why is it that no such part should be attributed directly to capital? As soon as it is understood and granted that capital is a factor of production, to the coöperation of which, with other causes, the result of the productive process must be ascribed, so soon will it be understood and granted that a part of the net returns in which that result is embodied is also due to capital. Should capital be supposed to be always able to produce only somewhat less than its own reimbursement? This assumption would evidently be arbitrary. Should it be assumed to produce always exactly its own reimbursement, however various the results of productive enterprises may be? This supposition would evidently be no less arbitrary. He who denies to capital a net return can do so only by denying returns to capital at all" (p. 124 *sq.*).

Here, I think, Wieser has taken the first

step from the right path. By the assumption that by way of imputation one may ascribe to a factor immediately some net return or some share in a net return, he has attributed to the operation of imputation something which by its very nature it cannot accomplish. Let us disregard all misleading words and hold ourselves strictly to the bare, dry facts of the case. What, according to Wieser himself, is the object and office of imputation? It is to distribute the result of production among the various factors coöperating in it, consequently to ascertain the share of each factor in the production of the gross product. Thus has Wieser himself repeatedly explained the problem of imputation in expressions quite unambiguous, and thus has he illustrated it by practical examples. So must it also necessarily be understood, if the method indicated by him for computing those shares (p. 87) is to be employed. If Wieser, for example, attributes the value of a tin vessel to the labour of the artisan and to the material out of which it is formed (p. 86), if in measuring the share of the produce belonging to land he takes his starting-point from the aggregate value of its produce (p. 113), if he assumes that the sum of all the productive contributions exhausts the value of the aggregate product (p. 87), and each factor derives its value from its productive contribution, it is perfectly evident that the thing to be imputed is the gross product and that the special contribution of the factor capital is and can be nothing else but an aliquot part of this gross product. If, for example, a husbandman, with the coöperation of labourers, and of capital composed of seed, agricultural implements, manure, live stock, etc., obtains from his land an aggregate product of 330 bushels of grain, it is the task of imputation to decide what portion of these 330 bushels is due to land, what to labourers, and what to the capital coöperating and in part worn out thereby. If this imputation happens to lead to the result that to each of the three factors the same share in producing the product is to be attributed, the productive contribution will be determined at 110 bushels for each, and it is perfectly evident that the 110 bushels ascribed to the coöperation of capital is a quota of gross returns. Whether in this quota of gross returns there will be found also a quota of net returns, likewise whether or not the portions of the gross product ascribed to land and labourers, from any point of view whatsoever, may be considered as net revenue, these are questions which go beyond the problem of imputation. For the solution of these questions the magnitude of the portions of gross returns imputed may be a relevant, even a very important element, but it can never form more than one single element, beside which other facts and considerations have an influence, though they have nothing to do with the process of imputation. In our example, the imputation ends with the statement that out of the gross product of 330 bushels the producer owes to each of the factors of production 110 bushels. Beyond this, imputation has not a single word to say.

But Wieser, nevertheless, thinks that he is able to make plausible the claim that a share even in the net revenue may be ascribed to capital by the process of imputation. But it is as interesting as it is significant, that he can only find the connecting link for his exposition by employing, unconsciously, of course, the term "net revenue" in a double sense. "Unquestionably," he says, in the passage above quoted, "the aggregate product of all the three factors of production, — land, labour, and capital together, is large enough to replace the capital consumed and to supply a net revenue!" Certainly, and this may be easily understood; for what is called "net revenue" in this sentence is the surplus of the aggregate product of land, labour, and capital above the value of the consumed capital alone, or, in other words, the surplus of the value of the product of three factors over that of one of them. But that three factors can produce more than one of them is worth, is not only a thing very plausible in itself, but becomes self-evident in connection with a theory which, like Wieser's, rests on the principle that the value of a product is identical with that of the sum of its factors. In the light of this principle the existence of the said "net revenue," is self-evident in the same degree as the axiom that the whole must be greater than one of its parts, or that a filled chest must have not only a "gross weight," but also a "net weight" beyond the weight of an empty chest.

It is thus clear that the reasons why, in the determination of that net return which results from production as a whole, the value of the capital consumed but not that of the consumed land and labour is deducted from the gross return, have nothing whatever to do with the question of imputation. It is well known that these reasons are rather to be found exclusively in the particular point of view from which the observer considers the outcome of production. If this point of view changes, the method of procedure in the matter of deducting or not deducting the value of those other factors of production also changes. For example, from his individual, economic standpoint, the employer who buys and pays for the labour of other people is certainly obliged to deduct from the gross product the value of the consumed labour also.[1] On the other hand, from the so-called

[1] Those who produce for their own account may also judge the success of production by considering whether the product of labour attains or exceeds the trouble of labour; if the utility

national economic standpoint,—the one which Wieser occupies when he says that more than a thousand millions of men are maintained out of these enormous net revenues,—that deduction must be omitted. But it is clear that the problem of imputation has absolutely nothing to do with the choice between these different standpoints and the corresponding methods of calculating the net revenue. How much of the gross product is to be attributed to the factor labour is one question, and that too a question of imputation; but whether or not one ought to deduct from the gross product the value of labour resulting from this computation is a completely different and an independent question.

Nevertheless Wieser wishes to utilize the existence of a net revenue of the above-described origin and nature in his explanation of the statement that a net revenue must be at-

which the labourer draws from his product is less than the trouble connected with the labour, one may say, from a point of view admissible and relevant, that labour is not remunerative. On the contrary, the surplus of utility over the trouble taken in its acquisition may be considered as a "net utility" (Marshall's "producer's surplus"; "Principles," 3d ed., p. 217).

tributed also to capital. As he puts it in the passage above quoted, only one question can be seriously asked, namely, whether a part of that unquestioned net revenue should also be attributed to the factor capital. "Why, then," he asks, "should no such share be attributed to capital?" The answer is very simple. Because what is called a "net return" from capital is no "such" net return at all, but a quantity of a very different nature, the existence of which depends on quite different and much more severe conditions. For, while a net product from the point of view above indicated is created as soon as the gross product of all the three factors together exceeds the value of the capital consumed, a net product of capital comes into existence only when the quota of the gross product assigned to the factor capital is greater than the capital consumed; and because there is so great diversity between the premises in the two cases, the realization of the first relation furnishes no probability or analogy in support of the conclusion that the second relation also must or will be realized. That three men together can lift more than the weight of one may be perfectly explicable and clear, but from this it by no means follows that one alone would be able to lift more than his own weight. It may be that he can, but he who wishes to maintain and at the same time to prove this will be obliged to allege some special cause having reference to that particular person; but such a cause can neither be derived from nor strengthened by the fact that three men together are able to lift more than the weight of one.

But if one destroys the fallacious bridge of explanation which Wieser constructs from net product in the one sense to net product in the other, no argument is left on which an explanation of the net revenue of capital could be based. When to the question, "Can the produce of capital only be something less than its own replacement," Wieser gives the answer, "This supposition would be perfectly arbitrary," he is quite right. But when he continues with the question, "Can the produce of capital only be as much as its own replacement, however various the results of productive processes may be," and answers, " This supposition would evidently be no less arbitrary," there is some doubt about the correctness of his statement; for it might well be that the returns of capital, according to the chance success of the individual undertaking, would fluctuate now above and now below the amount of the consumed capital, and yet on the average tend just to replace this amount. This assumption can scarcely appear arbitrary in connection with a theory like Wieser's which derives the value of a product from that of the factors which produced it. But even supposing this to be the case, yet from the arbitrary character of the two first assumptions the inference can never be drawn that the third supposition, namely, that capital must regularly produce more than its own replacement, is legitimate and justifiable, or that it may in this way be explained. It is no doubt an arbitrary supposition, that a man can always lift only something *less* than his own weight; it is equally arbitrary to suppose that he can lift *just* his own weight, neither more nor less; and in itself and without any other positive reason, it is certainly no less arbitrary to suppose that every man can lift more than his own weight. If, of three possible rules, two cannot be established, it by no means follows that the third fits the case, since the existence of any rule may remain in doubt. And if, in the case in question, from a source of knowledge totally different from such syllogisms, that is, from experience, we know that the share which must be attributed to capital is regularly greater than the capital consumed, yet no ray of light is shed on this fact by these syllogisms, which are not conclusive in themselves and contain no trace of an *explanation* such as every interest theory is called upon and bound to offer.

In what follows we also look in vain for anything of this kind. Wieser wishes to make his doctrine clear in a concrete case, and chooses the example of a machine which supplants hand-labour. "Wherever capital supplants hand-labour," he says, "where, for example, a machine does the work which up to that time has been done by hand, the capital, that is, the machine, must receive at least the amount previously attributed to the labour. That, however, was a net return; therefore, a net return must be attributed to capital also. That this syllogism likewise has no support except the above-criticised ambiguous use of the word net return, I need hardly tell the attentive reader. Here the non sequitur is still more striking. For a net return in the first sense, that is, in which the value of labour itself is not deducted from its product, might result from a very unprofitable, uneconomical employment of labour which does not cover the costs, and which therefore involves loss to the investor; an employment, for instance, in which labour to the value of 100 florins is consumed, but which adds a value of only about 50 florins to the raw material worked up. But who, following Wieser's method of reasoning, would be satisfied with the conclusion that the capital, which, with equal or somewhat more favourable results, takes the place of such labour, must receive not only a gross but also a net return, because, forsooth, it must receive at least the same return as the labour which it supplanted, and this was a "net return"?[1]

When, in a longer explanation, based upon Thünen's reasoning, Wieser further endeavours to make technically plausible the claim that capital must assist in the creation of a product in excess of its own substance, he strikes precisely the same rock upon which Thünen made shipwreck. Capital does not literally reproduce itself and something else in addition. It produces some other kinds of products, and these are commensurable with it only from the point of view of value. Bows and arrows do not produce bows and arrows, but dead game. The fact that this dead game is of greater value than the bow and arrow used up in its killing is not a technical fact which could be employed to explain the net profit of capital, — the object of the interest problem, — but is itself the thing to be explained.[2] Wieser himself also very clearly sees this difficulty. He distinctly adds that the product of bows and arrows is a "gross product in other kinds of

[1] "Der natürliche Wert," p. 125.

[2] See "Capital and Interest," Smart's translation, p. 169 *sq*.

goods, out of which they are not replaced, and with which they may be compared in value but not in quantity" (p. 130). But he believes that he is able to surmount this difficulty by means of a somewhat vague assumption of a "mediate efficiency (mittelbare Wirksamkeit) of capital." The possession of arrows, bows, and nets facilitates the conditions for reproduction, even though they do not contribute to it; it facilitates them by the extraordinary increase of the gross return in game and fish, in consequence of which far more labour than before is free for the production of capital. The final result, therefore, is that a net return is imputed to these capital goods, just as if they immediately reproduced themselves with a surplus.

In my opinion, there may possibly be some doubt whether this "mediate" connection is close and continuous enough to enable an exact computation to be based upon it. It might especially be doubted whether the technical commensurability between products which the labourer consumes and those which he will produce is not rather interrupted than mediated by the intercalation of the intermediary link, "person of the labourer"; for, if we except the case of slavery considered from the rudest slaveholder's standpoint, the working economic subject, as a factor of production on the one hand, represents an original productive force, and as a consumer on the other hand, represents the goal and final end of the productive endeavours which have gone before, so that his intervention seems to signify rather a cæsural pause in the technical process of production, a conclusion of previous efforts which attained their goal in his consumption and the beginning of a new production, rather than the continuation of one and the same productive process.

However, I will leave in abeyance this question, as delicate as it is difficult. Even if one does not wish to struggle with the manifold objections to which it leads, still the explanation proposed by Wieser would come to grief in the second part of his programme, that part which undertakes the task of deducing the value-productivity of capital from its physical productivity. Suppose that he has really succeeded in proving that to capital a concrete quantity of products must be ascribed which is greater than the quantity represented by the consumed capital itself, it still remains to be proved and explained that this greater quantity of produce must also have a greater value than the capital out of which it has arisen. This again is not at all self-evident, but in direct contradiction to the general premises of Wieser's imputation theory. Wieser's entire theory of value and imputation rests on the idea that the value of goods arises from the (marginal) utility to be attributed to them. This is true for production as well as for consumption goods. Now, production goods realize their utility through their products, and hence the utility which is ascribed to them is precisely the same as that ascribed to their products. Therefore, because a production good derives its value from the same quantity of utility as its product, it necessarily follows that it must have exactly the same value as that product. Consequently, provided no entirely new factor of special influence intervenes, a surplus of value in the product over and above that of its corresponding productive good or goods, or a value-productivity of capital, is entirely out of the question.

Wieser also sees this obstacle, to which I had called attention in my criticism of the older forms of the productivity theory,[1] and brings it clearly before his own eyes and those of his readers. "Capital," he says, "receives its value from its fruits; therefore, if you deduct . . . from the value of these fruits the value of the capital consumed, . . . no balance is left. . . . The amount deducted must always be as great as the value of these fruits, since these latter furnish the measure of the value of the quantity deducted. . . . Consequently the calculation of value furnishes no net return, and not only can interest not be explained by it, but it is proved to be quite impossible!" Wieser believes, however, that he has solved these difficulties by the results of his investigations regarding imputation. His imputation theory justifies him, he thinks, in attributing to capital not only a gross return, but also a physical net return. "In the gross product capital reproduces itself with a physi-

[1] See Smart's translation, p. 179.

cal surplus, the net product. Hence the value of capital cannot be rated equal to that of the gross product. In its reproduction capital forms but a part of its own gross product, consequently it can absorb only a part of the value of the gross product." If the gross product is worth 105, and a part equal to five be deducted for fruits which may be consumed without disturbing the complete replacement of capital, only "the remainder, 100, can be reckoned as the value of capital."[1]

To this argument two objections can be made. First of all, as I endeavoured to show above, one may contest the premise that the rules of imputation lead to the imputation of a physical net product to capital.[2] But even if this premise were correct, the conclusion drawn from it is not. Suppose we had really to attribute to a capital consisting of 100

[1] "Der natürliche Wert," pp. 134 *sq.* and 136.

[2] To avoid a misunderstanding, I wish to remark that Wieser maintains the "physical productivity of capital" in a sense which differs from all the numerous meanings of the term which I enumerated and explained in Section VII (p. 111 *sq.* of Smart's translation), and also from that recognized in my "Positive Theory" and made a support for a part of my exposition.

pieces of goods, a gross product of 105 pieces of the same kind and a net product of 5 pieces, the only conclusion which could be correctly drawn from this statement, in view of the universal law of the identity of the value of the means of production and of their products, is that the value of a single piece cannot be the same in both these generations of capital, but that 100 pieces of the earlier generation must be equivalent in value to 105 pieces of the following, *i.e.* the next year's generation. Thus evidently the value-equivalence of capital and its gross product would be maintained.

Indeed, Wieser can reach his opposite conclusion, that the value of capital can be estimated only at a smaller amount than that of its gross product, only by means of a deceptive logical blunder due to a dialectical trick. In this case he repeats a mistake already famous in the history of interest theories. Like the old canonists, together with their contemporary antagonists,[1] and like Knies in more recent times, Wieser imagines the identity of the original capital with an equal number of like

[1] See "Capital and Interest," Smart's translation, Ch. IX.

pieces of goods in a subsequent period. He introduces this fiction by a bit of dialectics. The fact, rightly or wrongly assumed, that a greater number of pieces than was contained in itself is assigned to capital as its share in the product, is expressed by Wieser in the words: "In the gross product capital reproduces itself with a physical surplus." From this basis, he proceeds step by step as follows: "In its reproduction capital represents only a part of its own product," and in consequence it cannot absorb more than a portion of the value of the gross product. In a more correct manner Wieser should have said in his first statement: "In the gross product capital produces an equal number of pieces of the same kind but available under other conditions of time and in addition a surplus of such pieces." The second sentence should then have read: "That equal number represents only a part of the gross product," and finally he could reach only the conclusion that that equal number could not absorb more than a portion of the value of the gross product. In short, it is clear and demonstrable that 100 pieces or units of the second generation of capital are worth less than 105 pieces of the same generation; but since the original capital of 100 pieces is by no means identical with the 100 pieces of the second generation, there is no justification for applying to the former the relation of value to gross product proved to exist in the latter. The truth, on the contrary, is that, as the general premises of Wieser's theory, to which the author has not remained quite true, postulate, capital is equivalent in value to its whole gross product, though this may consist of more pieces. How, in spite of this equivalent, an increment of value can arise which furnishes the material for interest, is the salient point of the interest problem. For this phenomenon, I believe, an explanation presents itself, if we take into account the influence of distance in time on the estimation of goods and the maturing of the future, originally less valued, goods into the full value of present goods;[1] whereas no satisfactory explanation can be found by sup-

[1] For a more explicit explanation see my "Positive Theory of Capital."

posing, contrary to principles, that productive goods in distinction from all others derive their value from a part only of the utility originated by them!

It is rather strange that in the further course of his inquiry Wieser also is led to the recognition of the central principle of my theory of interest, namely, that present goods as a rule are worth more than future ones. Only he is not willing to recognize this as a starting-point but as a conclusion of his demonstrations, not as a cause but as an effect of the phenomenon of interest.[1] However, if I am not wholly mistaken, this principle cannot be regarded as a deduction from Wieser's views, but must be considered incompatible with them. If a capital of 100 pieces gives in one year a gross product of 105 pieces, it cannot possibly at the same time be true that it possesses a value 5 per cent smaller than its gross product of 105

[1] "Yet it is not the same thing whether one possesses it (a capital) from the present moment or only a year hence, *because the present possession warrants one more term of interest. . . . A present sum is always superior in value to an equal sum due at a later term*" ("Der natürliche Wert," p. 138).

pieces, and yet is of the same value as 105 pieces of the ensuing year! Wieser could arrive at the latter conclusion,[1] in itself perfectly true, only by dropping here the fiction of the identity of present capital with a like number of pieces of its product. Only he ought not to have employed this fiction in his preceding arguments.

Wieser's theory of interest, expounded with much ingenuity and eloquence, is particularly interesting because it represents a peculiar attempt to attach to a system, modern through and through, an addition constructed out of old materials, namely, out of the "productivity of capital" which has so often appeared on the scene, and that venerable old fiction of the identity of the original capital with the "principal sum" which serves to replace it at some future period. This attempt, I believe, has not succeeded. The old and the new notions clash with each other. Thanks to the author's dialectical skill, the conflict of the new theories,

[1] In a substantially identical form it is to be found on page 138 ("Der natürliche Wert") in the statement that "100, which I shall obtain after a year only, are to-day worth but about 95."

—for the foundation of which Wieser himself has worked with lasting merit,—with the old were with difficulty concealed at the critical points; but the conflicting elements could not be brought into any intimate union. The failure of the attempt of a theorist of such force and resources to revive the productivity theory seems to me to be the best proof that the solution of the problem of interest can never be found in the process of thought peculiar to that theory.

CHAPTER VII

THE EXPLOITATION THEORY

During this entire period the exploitation theory has occupied much space in literary discussions. These have been especially excited and animated on account of a peculiar personal turn which they have taken and sometimes also on account of a kind of dramatic tension. Of all socialistic writers Karl Marx — not perhaps without an unjust depreciation of others, and especially of Rodbertus, whose scientific rank was high — had gained the greatest influence over his partisans. His work represented, so to speak, the official doctrine of contemporary socialism. It therefore occupied the centre of attack and defence. The polemical literature of the time became a literature on Marx. The circumstances also were of unusual interest. Marx had died before he had brought his work on capital to an end. The unfinished parts were found in manuscript among his belongings in an almost complete form. These were expected to furnish the explanation of a problem which had been the chief cause of the attack against the exploitation theory and which, according to the expectations of both the contending parties, would furnish the deciding test of the tenableness or untenableness of the Marxian system, the problem, namely, of harmonizing and connecting the rate of profits, which experience shows tends toward equality in all forms of investment, with the law of value and the theory of exploitation which Marx had developed in his first volume.[1] The publication of the third volume, in which this theme was treated, was delayed until 1894, eleven years after the death of Marx. The interest in the question regarding what Marx himself might have had to say on this most delicate point of his theory showed itself in a sort of prophetic literature which had for its object the development of Marx's probable opinion on the subject of the average rate of profit from the premises given

[1] See "Geschichte und Kritik der Capitalzins-Theorien," 2d ed., Section XII, p. 530 *sq*.

in his first volume. This prophetic literature fills the decade from 1885–1894, and presents a stately array of more or less extensive publications.[1] The second act and at the same time the climax of the dramatic development was reached in 1894 by Engels's publication of the posthumous third volume. And then follows as a third act an exceedingly animated literary discussion on the critical estimate of this third volume, its relation to the point of

[1] I have given a compilation of these on another occasion (in an essay "Zum Abschluss des Marx'schen Systems," in the "Festgaben für Carl Knies," 1896, p. 6). It comprises: Lexis, *Jahrbücher für Nationalökonomie*, 1885, N.F., Vol. XI, pp. 452–465; Schmidt, "Die Durchschnittsprofitrate auf Grund des Marx'schen Wertgesetzes," Stuttgart, 1889; an examination of this latter paper by myself in the *Tübinger Zeitschrift f. d. ges. Staatsw.*, 1890, p. 590 *sq.*, and by Loria in the *Jahrbücher für Nationalökonomie*, N.F., Vol. XX (1890), p. 272 *sq.*; Stiebeling, "Das Wertgesetz und die Profitrate," New York, 1890; Wolf, "Das Räthsel der Durchschnittsprofitrate bei Marx," *Jahrbücher für Nationalökonomie*, III F., Vol. 2 (1891), p. 352 *sq.*; again Schmidt, *Neue Zeit*, 1892–1893, Nos. 4 and 5; Landé, *ibid.*, Nos. 19 and 20; Fireman, "Kritik der Marx'schen Werttheorie," *Jahrbücher für Nationalökonomie*, III F., Vol. 3 (1892), p. 793 *sq.*; finally, Lafargue, Soldi, Coletti, and Graziadei, in the *Critica Sociale*, from July to November, 1894. Of the other literature of this period on Marx, we may refer to Georg Adler, "Die Grundlagen der Karl Marx'schen Kritik der bestehenden Volkswirtschaft," Tübingen, 1887.

departure taken by Marx in the systematic development of his theories, and the future prospects of Marxism, a discussion which is not likely soon to reach a conclusion.[1]

I can content myself here with a mere registration of these events, because in an earlier part of this work I have described their scientific content and subjected them to a critical analysis. Nor have I withheld my opinion

[1] Of the writings on this subject which have hitherto appeared may be mentioned: numerous essays in the *Neue Zeit*, especially by Engels (XIV Jahrgang, Vol. 1, Nos. 1 and 2), Bernstein, and Kautsky; then Loria, "L'opera posthuma di Carlo Marx" (*Nuova Antologia*, February, 1895); Sombart, "Zur Kritik des ökonomischen Systems, von K. Marx" (*Archiv für soc. Gesetzgebung und Statistik*, Vol. VII, Pt. 4); the above-mentioned essay by myself, "Zum Abschluss des Marx'schen Systems," 1896; Komorzynsky, "Der dritte Band von Carl Marx, 'das Kapital,'" in the *Zeitschr. für Volkswirthschaft, Socialpolitik und Verwaltung*, Bd. VI, p. 242 *sq.*; Wenkstern, "Marx," Leipzig, 1896; Diehl, "Ueber das Verhältnis von Wert und Preis im ökonomischen System von Carl Marx" (in the "Festschrift zur Feier des 25 jährigen Bestehens des staatsw. Seminars in Halle," Jena, 1898); Labriola, "La teoria del valore di Carl Marx," Milan, 1899; Graziadei, "La produzione capitalistica," Turin, 1899; Bernstein, "Die Voraussetzungen des Socialismus und die Aufgaben der Socialdemokratie," Stuttgart, 1899; Masaryk, "Die philosophischen und sociologischen Grundlagen des Marxismus," Vienna, 1899; Weisengrün, "Das Ende des Marxismus," Leipzig, 1899.

that the great test has been decidedly against Marx and his theories of value and surplus value, and that for these the beginning of the end seems to be at hand.

But the period under discussion presents us with another very peculiar theoretical development which must be mentioned in this connection, and which I have called in another place the "vulgär-ökonomischen" branch of the socialistic theory of exploitation.[1] This peculiar phenomenon may be described as follows: Various eminent theorists of a non-socialistic tendency, who do not even recognize the theoretical value-premises of the socialistic exploitation theory, have yet adopted a general view of interest which in its essence is identical with the exploitation theory and differs from it only in its more moderate, more reserved, or less consistent form.

The most characteristic expressions of this kind come from Dietzel and Lexis. Dietzel confesses it to be his opinion that in its

[1] "Einige strittige Fragen der Capitalstheorie," Vienna, 1900, p. 111. (Also printed in Vol. VIII of the *Zeitschrift für Volkswirtschaft, Socialpolitik und Verwaltung.*)

essence the exploitation theory is undeniable, and maintains that he is obliged to accept the view that the interest phenomenon is a historical product which is rooted in the commercial law of the present time, and that it is one of those kinds of income which in a form of society like the present are justly blamed as necessarily opposed to the maxim *suum cuique*.[1] Lexis expresses the opinion that the normal profit on capital is connected with the relations of power brought about by the possession or non-possession of capital. The source of the slave-holder's profits is unmistakable, and the same may be said of the profits of the "sweater." In the normal relation of the employer to the workman there exists no exploitation of this kind, but an economic dependence of the workman which undoubtedly influences the division of the product of labour. The share of the workman in the yield of production is conditioned by the circumstance, unfavourable to him, that he cannot utilize his working power independently, but is compelled to sell it,

[1] *Göttinger Gelehrte Anzeigen*, No. 23, 1891, pp. 935, 943.

resigning his claim to the product for a more or less adequate means of subsistence.[1] On another occasion Lexis still more clearly explains this opinion of his on the origin of interest by saying that the capitalistic seller, the producer of raw material, the manufacturer, the wholesale dealer, the retailer, make profits in their business by selling at a higher price than they buy, thereby raising the cost price of their goods by a certain per cent. The labourer alone is unable to get a similar advance of price. On account of his unfavourable situation with reference to the capitalist he is compelled to sell his labour at the price which it costs himself, namely, the necessary means of subsistence. Thus, even if capitalists by buying goods at a higher price lose again a part of what they win as sellers, these advanced prices retain their full significance for the wage-earner who buys, and effects the transfer of part of the value of the total product to the capitalist class.[2]

In all these statements the idea is unmis-

[1] Schmoller's *Jahrbuch*, Vol. XIX, p. 335 *sq*.

[2] Conrad's *Jahrbücher*, N.F., Vol. XI (1885), p. 453.

takably expressed that profits — and not merely some excessive portion acquired under especially burdensome circumstances, but ordinary, normal profits as such — arise from the pressure which the possessing classes exert on the non-possessing by availing themselves of the stronger position which they hold in the struggle for price, an idea which is essentially the same as that which forms the essence of the socialistic theory of exploitation.

In order to characterize these statements, attention should be called to two circumstances which may bear some relation to each other. The first is that up to the present time they have been presented as occasional statements only, and have been made on occasions which prompted the authors to a confession of their own opinions on the interest problem, but did not force them to a systematic defence and explanation of their views, namely, on the occasion of a critical review of other people's theories (Marx's and my own). The second circumstance is that these statements have presented themselves hitherto only as simple expressions of opinion, as confessions of faith of the authors, for which a connected, theoretically tenable foundation has neither been given nor attempted. Dietzel does not add a word in support of his statements, and the brief remarks[1] with which Lexis accompanies the expression of his opinion are so vague and leave the problem so plainly unexplained that the author himself will hardly claim that they contain, even in general outlines, a really adequate explanation.

In view of the fact that the theoretical grounds upon which the views of the exploitation theorists are usually based, namely, the socialistic theories of value and surplus value, are not laid down by these authors as a basis for their allied theory of interest, and in view of the fact that till now no other tenable foun-

[1] Namely, that, even under the full pressure of competition, — which is the condition necessary to the levelling of profits to the normal rate, — capitalistic sellers are yet able permanently to maintain a surplus of value above prime costs, and that this is the peculiar fact which requires an explanation such as will be compatible with the laws of value and price, or such as may be plausibly deduced from them. Yet there is nothing in what Lexis says to suggest the existence of these facts. Consult the exhaustive treatment of this subject in my above-mentioned essay, "Einige strittige Fragen der Capitalstheorie," Vienna, 1900, p. 110 *sq.*

dation has been laid for it, as a historian of doctrines I have merely to register the fact that these opinions exist, and that for the present, at least, they exist merely as unproved non-theoretical statements. We must wait to see whether an earnest attempt will be made to elevate these confessions of faith to real theories based upon some kind of a foundation, or whether they will die out as mere expressions of feeling to which the tendency of the time inclines without any attempt to bring them into connection with tenable scientific premises.[1]

[1] I have expressed myself more completely upon this peculiar branch of the exploitation theory in my oft-mentioned essay, "Einige strittige Fragen der Capitalstheorie." A somewhat older attempt to bring the exploitation theory into connection with a value theory differing from the socialistic one may be found in Wittelshöfer's "Untersuchungen über das Capital," Tübingen, 1890. This attempt is interesting, but in my opinion not profound.

CHAPTER VIII

THE ECLECTICS

By no means inconsiderable in the most recent times is the number or the importance of those theorists who base their explanation of interest in an eclectic way on elements of different theories. As I have taken the opportunity on a previous occasion to say, this is not to be wondered at.[1] One can scarcely fail to recognize the truth, which has been very clearly brought to view by the most recent investigations in this field, that more than one group of facts stand in a casual relation with interest. Especially is this the case with the greater fruitfulness of capitalistic production on the one hand, and of the postponement of gratification connected with every investment of capital on the other. On each of these two points independent theories have been founded, and as long as no outcome in the form of a

[1] See "Capital and Interest," Smart's translation, p. 396.

solution appeared, or was acknowledged as such, which permitted one to view the interworkings of these heterogeneous half causes from one single point of view, authors of broad vision who do not close their eyes to any of the facts of experience are easily led to an eclectic combination.

I have already spoken of Loria, who combined elements of the abstinence with those of the exploitation theory.[1] Diehl combines a sort of indirect productivity theory with considerations and expressions peculiar to the use theory.[2] Modes of expression characteristic of the latter theory are found in Sidgwick side by side with arguments which expound and defend the abstinence theory.[3] On this account I think it likely that the modes of expression which reflect the spirit of the use theory are employed in a merely incidental manner, and that the real opinion of that distinguished writer is actually represented by the abstinence theory.

[1] See above, Ch. IV.

[2] P. J. Proudhon, "Seine Lehre und sein Leben," Pt. II, Jena, 1890, pp. 217–225, and p. 204.

[3] "Principles of Political Economy," 2d ed., London, 1887, pp. 167, 168, 255 *sq.*, and 264.

Neurath's somewhat vague expressions do not indicate any clearly worked-out theory, but rather a partial agreement with or inclination toward a whole series of traditional methods of explanation.[1] I do not believe that I shall meet with opposition, if I place the learned and intellectual author of "Progrès de la Science Économique depuis Adam Smith," Maurice Block, among the eclectics. As a convinced believer in the complete justification of interest, he could not make up his mind to abandon any of the numerous conceptions which seemed to him equally plausible and favourable to interest. In his copious disquisitions on that subject I find the productivity theory represented as well as the abstinence and the use theories.[2] That for the eminent scholar himself the thought of being considered an eclectic had no terrors is proved by an earnest plea, doubtless intended as an *oratio pro domo*, which he once made in favour of eclecticism.[3]

[1] "Elemente der Volkswirtschaftslehre," 2d ed., Vienna, 1892, pp. 282 *sq.*, 313 *sq.*, and 324 *sq.*

[2] See "Progrès" (Paris, 1890), Vol. II, pp. 319, 320, 328, 335 *sq.*; also pp. 321, 326, 339, 340–342, and 348.

[3] *Ibid.*, p. 334; see also p. 349.

Charles Gide's expressions seem to me to lean partly toward the use and partly toward the agio theory,[1] Nicholson's partly toward the agio and partly toward the abstinence theory.[2] The latter combination appears rather frequently in recent times, as I have shown in Chapters II and IV.

Among the authors inclined to eclecticism Dietzel occupies a special place. This always intellectual, but not always coolly reflective, author, in a detailed review of my theory of interest, has acknowledged himself to be an eclectic on principle, in the sense that he regards the different current theories of interest, especially the exploitation and productivity theories taken together, as pertinent and applicable each to a part of the phenomenon of interest. He thinks that "in the field of interest different explanations, conditioned by the difference in the economic positions and relations of individuals, should be formulated for the different categories of socio-economic phe-

1 "Principes d'Économic Politique," 5th ed., p. 451, footnote.

2 "Principles of Political Economy," London, 1893–1897; see especially Vol. I, p. 388, and Vol. II, pp. 217 and 219.

nomena." For example, if the hirer of a piano or a house possesses a capital large enough for the purchase of the piano or house, yet prefers to invest or leave it in a productive undertaking, the interest which the possessor of the house or piano receives may be fittingly explained by the productivity of capital. If, however, the tenant does not possess capital sufficient to buy the hired object, then the interest could only be explained as an exploitation of the tenant, and the "exploitation theory (undeniable in its essence) becomes the explanation of interest."[1] Dietzel also defends the use theory,[2] and finally, if I have correctly understood him, grants to my theory of interest justification for a certain group of interest phenomena, namely, for the explanation of interest in the case of credit granted for purposes of consumption.[3]

As I fully explained in another place[4] not long ago, I consider Dietzel's point of view regarding methods as very unfortunate and

[1] *Göttinger Gelehrte Anzeigen*, 1891, No. 23, p. 930 *sq.*, especially pp. 932–935.

[2] *Ibid.*, p. 933.

[3] *Ibid.*, p. 932 *sq.*

[4] "Einige strittige Fragen der Capitalstheorie," Vienna, 1900, p. 84 *sq.*

quite untenable. Something may indeed be said against eclecticism of every kind. Still it makes a great difference whether, as eclectics have been accustomed to do, one invents for the explanation of a phenomenon a theory in which incoherent elements of different theories are combined into an external unity, or whether, as Dietzel desires, for each group of instances of one and the same phenomenon one works out or recognizes a totally new and fundamentally different theory. If that form of income, which economists are accustomed to comprehend under the head of interest or rent of capital, in contradistinction to rent of land, wages of labour, and profits of the entrepreneur, has anything really characteristic about it which binds together the cases belonging under this head and separates them from the other sorts of income, then that characteristic something cannot possibly be different in every case, certainly not fundamentally different and even contradictory. Nevertheless, he who, with Dietzel, attempts to explain instances of the same fundamental phenomenon by means of contrasting theories, in the first place cannot avoid getting entangled in absurd inferences; as, for example, Dietzel, when he concludes that the possessor of a house who in two succeeding years lets the same luxurious dwelling for 2000 florins, one year to the manager of a bank with a salary of 15,000 florins, and the second year to a manufacturer with an income from property of 15,000 florins, owes his interest in the first case to exploitation and in the second to the productivity of capital! In the second place, he cannot avoid entanglement in the most obvious contradictions, since each contrasting theory contains premises which we must acknowledge if we wish to explain a single instance in the spirit of that theory, and which are in complete opposition to the premises of other theories which it would be likewise necessary to recognize in order to explain other instances according to Dietzel's plan. Can any one who regards the exploitation theory as essentially correct explain any given case of interest in the spirit of the productivity theory or vice versa? In my opinion, Dietzel has been able to escape these palpable inconveniences only because he, perhaps rather hastily, announced his maxim in the capacity of a critic instead of that of a systematic exponent of doctrines, and therefore had no occasion to attempt to put its applicability to a practical test.

CHAPTER IX

THE PRESENT STATE OF OPINION

THUS even in our days very many and very different opinions are struggling for mastery. The final issue of the struggle is certainly not yet decided. But the battle has not remained stationary. Many an undoubted success and many an undoubted defeat have been witnessed on this vast field of conflict. Certain views have clearly pushed into the foreground and are advancing, while others are retreating or are engaged in a difficult defence of some unfavourable position in the rear, the strongest fortifications of which have already fallen. If I should venture to draw a picture of the present state of the combat as it appears to me, I would draw the lines as follows:—

On one of the main fronts of the many-sided and much-divided battlefield the exploitation theory on one side has been fighting with the different theories favourable to interest on the other. Here the issue seems to me to be no longer doubtful. The exploitation theory is vanquished. On account of the compulsory abandonment of the theory of value upon which it was based, it has been forced into an untenable position. To be sure the battle will be continued for a time by its adherents, and the dogma of exploitation will not be likely soon to vanish from that part of the party platforms designed for purposes of agitation. But science will probably soon place it forever in the list of errors which have finally been overcome. The "vulgär-ökonomische" branch of this theory, of which we have spoken, can hardly possess sufficient motive power to be able to regenerate and fruitfully to develop the dying doctrine.

The conflict between the rival theories which are favourable to interest, if I may use this brief but not fully adequate phrase for theories unassociated with parties, has not remained without lasting results. I think that nowadays it may be considered as a recognized truth that the final causes of the phenomenon of interest are to be found on the one hand in certain facts of the technique of production, and on the other in the postponement of enjoyment, precisely or very nearly as Professor Marshall has expressed himself in his popular catchwords, the "prospectiveness" and the "productiveness" of capital. Those branches of theory which stand outside of this truth or are not affected by it in the course of their explanations do not seem to me to enjoy any prospect that a backward movement will turn the course of development into the side path which they now occupy. This is the case, I think, with several varieties of labour theories and with the genuine, outspoken productivity theories. These latter particularly, which once played such an important rôle in economic theory, viewed from our modern standpoint, have two principal defects which are daily becoming more and more generally recognized and acknowledged. They cannot reach their goal by a logical path without turning a logical somersault, and without leaving completely out of consideration a full half of the actual causes of the phenomenon of interest. It seems to me to be a distinctive symptom of the hopeless condition of these theories that attempts have lately been made, — as I think, in violation of the actual condition of things and of historical truth, — entirely to deny their existence and to impute to their representatives other ideas which more nearly approach modern views of the problem.[1]

The most vigorous part of the development tends by common consent toward one goal, the correctness of the choice of which, at least as an object of knowledge, only a few at the present time will doubt; and which will surely be reached sooner or later, however much one may waver and hesitate regarding the choice of the most direct route thereto. The aim is to find an explanation so appropriate to both groups of causes, — the productive-technical facts and the psychological facts connected with the postponement of gratification, — that not only every part of the explanation will be in itself incontestable from the standpoint both of facts and of logic, but that both halves of the explanation will constitute a whole, formally and logically faultless.

[1] See my Preface to the 2d ed. of "Capital and Interest."

Of the different theories which are rivals in the struggle for the attainment of this goal the use theory is one to which it must be conceded that, correctly and completely understood, it is connected with both groups of causes, and is, therefore, sufficiently comprehensive; but in the course of its explanations it encounters weighty objections in the realms of both fact and logic, which it seems to me are at the present time being felt and appreciated as such in ever widening scientific circles.

The abstinence theory also finds difficulties of fact and of logic in the method of explanation it has adopted. These I have tried in the above pages to make more distinct than hitherto, and on this point it seems to me that the manner in which they attempt to do justice to "productiveness" side by side with "prospectiveness," which gives the characteristic stamp to their explanation, is not calculated to lead to a happy coalescence into a really united theory.

The eclectics naturally have to contend with the special weaknesses of each theory taken into the eclectic combination as well as with the resistance of the incongruous elements to coalescence into a harmonious whole.

Since the time of Rae the postponement of gratification has been understood in a way which is free from the objectionable interpretations of the abstinence theory. Yet in the second part of his explanation Rae remained entangled in the mistakes of thought and assumption characteristic of the productivity theories. Jevons again was more fortunate in this second part, but less so in the treatment of "prospectiveness," since he here turned back into the paths of the abstinence theorists, and altogether missed the prime requisite of a logically harmonious combination of the different grounds of explanation.

The youngest member in the series of rival interest theories, the agio theory, has made an experiment, which, however its outcome may be regarded, has at least aimed to keep clearly and consciously before our eyes the goal to be attained, namely, a coherent explanation of the phenomenon of interest derived from a comprehensive consideration of all the final causes which have an influence upon it.

No one will doubt that it has remained true to the first part of the programme. A characteristic piece of evidence regarding the comprehensive consideration it has given to both "productiveness" and "prospectiveness" is the fact that some of the friends of these ideas have accompanied their approval of the "agio theory" with the remark that it is in its essence a theory of productivity, and others again with the remark that it is really an abstinence theory.[1] Perhaps a still more striking bit of evidence along this line is a certain reproof expressed by one of my most prominent adversaries. When Professor Marshall reproaches me with attaching an exaggerated importance to the differences of opinion of my predecessors in the theory of interest, and in proof calls attention to the fact that the consideration of "prospectiveness" and "productiveness" as of

[1] In a detailed review of my "Positive Theory" in *De Economist*, March, 1889, p. 217, Pierson says: "Our author stands wholly on the ground of the productivity theory." Macfarlane, on the other hand, denotes a special paragraph (107) of his work "Value and Distribution" to the demonstration of the proposition that "abstinence is recognized in the exchange theory."

equal importance is to be found in their expressed views, it is evident that he regards this method of treatment as common to both doctrines, and is consequently by no means inclined to deny it to mine.

Whether the agio theory has also been successful in the second part of the programme, or at least more successful than its rivals, will be made evident in the continued discussion of the subject. The closer the results of previous investigation and criticism have drawn the lines within which the paths leading to the goal must be sought and laid out, the more careful in the future will be the search and the investigation within this region. We know our way approximately, or, as J. B. Clark, perhaps somewhat optimistically but not entirely incorrectly, said not long ago in an inspiring survey of the "Future of Economic Theory": "Explanations of interest *that cannot be far from the truth* have been offered."[1]

From now on the problem will be to test the different paths which we have been invited to take by the rival theories of the present day,

[1] *Quarterly Journal of Economics*, October, 1898, p. 1.

as to their direct and continuous connection with the goal toward which we are travelling. This test must be applied with more boldness, severity, and discrimination, than formerly, since we already possess sufficient orientation of the casual sort, and no further directions of a roundabout and not strictly accurate character can at the present time advance us on our way. Whatever may be the final outcome of this critical development of doctrine in the future, one thing seems to me already certain, namely, that the now awakened critical spirit will not be content with any solution which does not satisfy the severest scientific demands, and that the danger that rest may be found in one of those shallow solutions which are easily embodied in convenient catchwords but cannot be systematically thought out to the end, is forever past.

INDEX OF AUTHORS MENTIONED

[1] The letter *n* appended to page numbers refers to the foot-note at bottom of page.

Made in the USA
Monee, IL
04 November 2026

67384628R00108